the s.p.a.r.k. effect

A FRAMEWORK *REDEFINING* LEADERSHIP OF THE FUTURE

DR. MICHELLE BROWN

ISBN: 979-8-9996585-0-0

DEDICATION

To the One who goes before me and lights every path—this is for You, God. Thank You for being my source for planting this book in my spirit, my strength, and the steady foundation through every set back, every valley and each victory.

To my husband, Coach Patrick Brown—as much of a coach and mentor on the football field for athletes, you are also my coach and mentor in friendship, in partnership, and life. Your love grounds me and your nonstop belief in me fuels me. Thank you for walking beside me intentionally, standing in purpose and moving in union.

To my children—you are my greatest legacy and generational carrier. May you always know your worth, walk in your calling, and rise with boldness without fear. This work is a seed planted for you, so you may ignite the paths along your journeys to even greater heights.

To my ancestors and elders—especially my grandparents, Marine Sgt. Victor Bañuelos and Grace Bañuelos, and great-grandparents Carlos and Lupe Bañuelos, who journeyed here as Native immigrants to the U.S.—your courage, sacrifice, and dreams are etched into every fiber of my being. You carried hope across borders, labored in unfamiliar lands, and created a foundation from faith, grit, and community. I am because you were. Your legacy is alive in me, and it is my honor to carry it forward.

To my close circle of friends and loyal prayer warriors—thank you for standing in the gap, interceding when I couldn't find the words, and speaking life into my spirit when I needed it most. Your love, truth, and unwavering faith carried me further than you know.

To every leader who ever doubted their power, questioned their purpose, or felt unseen—this is your reminder: **You were born to rise.** May this book awaken your **S.P.A.R.K.**, ignite your vision, and reaffirm that transformation starts within.
And to every generation that follows—**may you lead with love, live with courage, and never dim your light to fit a broken system.** This is the solution and shift we've been waiting for.

CONTENTS

INTRODUCTION

For as long as I can remember, I have woken up every morning knowing exactly what I was going to do and how I was going to do it. That is, until one random day I wondered *why* we wake up each day and do the same thing, time and time again without question. Have you ever felt like your days were stale? For me, I started to wake up feeling like something was missing. But I could not pinpoint what it was.

Eventually, I let it go and moved through my daily routine without question. But the tension never faded. Then suddenly, enough was enough. I was tired of waking up and checking emails before I even got out of bed. I felt anxiety from the day's demand already in full force. My chest tightened with thoughts of having to perform, produce, and prove my value to others around me.

On paper, I was "thriving." Inside, I was exhausted and empty. That's when I started to realize that my spark had faded. Have you ever felt your spark dim too?

We live in a world that glorifies hustle, speed, and endless achievement. Everywhere you turn, someone is offering a new formula for success. It is often one that demands sacrifice regarding your peace, values, or identity. But here's what outdated leadership playbooks won't tell you: The very internal systems that got us here are the internal same systems keeping us stuck.

And the cost of staying stuck is only getting higher every day.

The industrial age scaled with models that exerted command-and-control leadership, compartmentalized thinking that separates personal growth from professional excellence, and reactive approaches that mistake motion for progress. Such frameworks aren't solely ineffective anymore; they're destructive. These approaches only fuel high anxiety environments in which we no longer function in purpose.

Organizations that use them satisfy the individuals seeking to develop themselves within their professional life. These approaches threaten the core of who each person is and create space for them to simply exist with no growth goal in mind.

In turn, we chase productivity at the expense of purpose. Yet, when we trade presence for pace, we risk building lives and careers that are high functioning, while remaining hollow and purposeless. And I recognize that is what caused my spark to go out.

I was trapped in survival mode that was dressed up as performance and false validation of my worth.

In case I am not alone, and you are like me, I want to invite you to ditch operating on outdated internal systems—and move toward becoming a leader who understands the new rules, and these new rules are simple.

These include:

New Leadership Rules	What It Means / Looks Like
Human-Centered **and** Human-Focused	You see your people as humans first, roles second. You pay attention to their emotions, capacity, and lived experience when making decisions.
Be Personable **and** Professional	You bring warmth, authenticity, and relatability into your leadership, while still maintaining clear boundaries, integrity, and standards.
Lead **and** Be Led	You don't hoard authority. You invite input, share power, and allow your team's expertise and feedback to shape direction and decisions.
Honor human needs for breaks **while** maintaining excellence	You normalize rest, recovery, and sustainable pacing, while still holding a high bar for quality, accountability, and follow-through.
Be Stern **and** Agile	You are clear, direct, and firm about expectations and values, yet flexible in how goals are reached and willing to adapt as circumstances change.
Co-exist **and** Create **CoEvolution™**	You build an organizational culture where leaders and teams grow together while learning from each other, adjusting together, and evolving in response to new realities, no matter what it "looks" like.

Striking the balance set in these new leadership rules is not easy. But it is vital.

I've learned through both experience and transformation: The more the world accelerates, the more essential it becomes to slow down and consider which framework we are operating out of. Speed without grounding becomes chaos in disguise. When we slow down, we don't lose our edge, instead we are sharpening it. I have come to value trading my own constant reactivity for clear, informed thinking. I am giving up making rushed decisions for choosing wise ones. I want to eradicate chronic tension and instead seek to have a steady, grounded presence that my team can trust.

And I welcome you to join me.

What feels like a "risk" to abandon these familiar patterns is actually the safest choice you can make for you and your future. On the other side of slowing down is better judgment, deeper connection with your people, and more meaningful work. It is the path to performance that's sustainable instead of exhausting. This is your invitation to abandon the internal systems that no longer serve the complexity of our world, the needs of our people, or the pace of our human evolution, and instead come on a journey to find your **S.P.A.R.K.** again.

"Your spark was never lost—it was buried beneath outdated systems, survival mode, and noise. Chapter 1 is where you begin uncovering the leader you were always meant to become."

CHAPTER 1– THE FOUNDATION
STAYING GROUNDED TO SOAR

WE ARE HUMAN, NOT LABELS

When I realized my life had turned into nonstop performance-mode as soon as I woke up each day, I noticed something unsettling. Somewhere along the way, I had started to confuse who I am as a human being with what I do. I introduced myself with titles. I measured my worth with outcomes. I tried to be the version of me that would disrupt the least so I could avoid any ripple effect that wasn't favorable. I shrank myself to please other professionals and leaders and fit the expectations of whatever room I walked into. The more I tried to be "enough" for everyone else, the further I drifted from my own center.

Maybe you feel it too—the sense that your identity is a role, a résumé, or a responsibility more than a full human. You're "the leader," "the high performer," "the reliable one," "the only one like you in the room." You embody the label, but people don't get to see *you*.

For example:

When the political climate and landscape changes, we may not have government power over what's to come, but we do have the power to pivot and stay grounded in our "why," our organization's mission and vision, and our personal values. This isn't just about adapting to external changes—it's about taking proactive action to create the internal systems and approaches that can thrive regardless of external circumstances.

If you've never set intentional strategic goals, you'll always operate from scarcity and reaction instead of strategy and planning that allows you to pivot and move with purpose. If you've never challenged the fundamental assumptions underlying your current approaches, you'll always be limited by internal systems designed for someone else's success and from a completely different era.

Often, organizations and leaders are more concerned with chasing trends than focusing on the true driver behind all business and this world: the people they serve. They take action that looks progressive—implementing new technologies, launching new initiatives, adopting new methodologies—while leaving the underlying internal systems and cultures completely unchanged.

Prioritizing short-term goals over long-term impact yields negative ROI and poor client satisfaction. Taking action that maintains comfortable patterns, while avoiding systematic transformation, yields the illusion of progress while ensuring continued limitation.

I want you to find the path to reclaiming that *you, again*.

It's time to name that truth and discover that we are more than any title, category, or checkbox. We do not have to cut off parts of ourselves just to fit outdated professional molds. Instead, we can lead, work, and live from a more honest, integrated place without separating what makes us who we are as a professional.

That's why I want you to hear this clearly:

We are human. We are not labels, checkboxes, or one-size-fits-all identities. We are mothers, fathers, brothers, sisters, colleagues, grandparents, leaders, professionals, nurses, doctors, social workers, coaches, and more. We are dreamers, disruptors, nurturers, and legacy builders.

The same human who shows up at home also shows up in the workplace—and vice versa. Authentic leadership embraces every dimension of who we are, instead of fragmenting ourselves to fit outdated professional molds. Leadership that lasts must reflect the fullness of who we are as humans—not just the roles we play as professionals.

Therefore, we need a framework and leadership model that is human-centered first, data-informed, and practical enough to shape how we build teams, design internal systems, and make everyday decisions that help us pivot with ease. Modern workstyles require a framework that doesn't ask us to choose between results and humanity but shows us how to create both.

That is exactly why we created the **S.P.A.R.K. Framework™**—a human-centered blueprint for leaders (with or without titles) who are ready to fix what's broken, build realistic ecosystems from the inside out, and lead with clarity in a world that demands holistic approaches for a world that will continue to keep changing.

This book isn't about identifying more problems or analyzing what's broken. You already know what's not working. This is about the solutions that create lasting transformation— real solutions that are human centered by design, yet strategically leverage AI and technology as powerful allies, not replacements.

Let's discover how.

THE S.P.A.R.K. FRAMEWORK™ – Redefining Leadership

You don't have to lose yourself to rise. In fact, you rise because you're grounded in who you are, but grounding alone isn't enough. In a world of constant change, you also need internal systems, language, and structures that actually support that kind of leadership.

That's where the **S.P.A.R.K. Framework™** comes in.

This is more than a set of ideas—it's a movement for leaders who are done with burnout, noise, and quick fixes, and who are ready to build internal systems that put humans back at the center. When I say "leaders," I don't just mean the C-suite. Whether you have an official title or not, if you influence anyone—at home, at work, in your community, online, or in your circle—you are a leader.

In this book, you'll find both personal truths and professional strategies to enhance your best next step as an individual, a professional, a leader of a team, and an organization. The **S.P.A.R.K. Framework™** is more than a concept—it's a mirror and a map. You'll be provided scenarios for leaders, coaches, and consultants that you can refer to and apply actionable next steps in your own organizations. You will also be invited to reflect, reassess, and redefine your mindset, thinking, approaches, and outdated internal systems so that you can:

- Lead with clarity instead of confusion.
- Build internal systems that speak *human*, not just "policy or procedure."
- Break out of autopilot and move into aligned action.

Now, let's see how:

The **S.P.A.R.K. Framework™**—**[S]**trategy, **[P]**lanning, **[A]**ction, **[R]**esults, and **[K]**PI Knowledge—isn't just for boardrooms or business plans.

It's for everyday real life.

[S]trategy helps you define where you're going and why—so that your goals align with your values, not just your vanity metrics.

[P]lanning helps you turn vision into a grounded, realistic path—so that you stop living in crisis mode and start leading with intention.

[A]ction directs your energy toward what actually moves the needle—so that you're not just busy, you're effective.

[R]esults help you see what's really working and what isn't—so that you can celebrate wins, learn from misses, and adjust without shame.

[K]PI Knowledge helps you measure what matters most—so that data informs your decisions without defining your identity.

This isn't a tool for mindset *alone*. It's a holistic, human-centered ecosystem that touches how you think, how you design internal systems, how you show up in relationships, and how you measure success—both personally and professionally.

To help guide this process, throughout this book, you'll see QR codes which provide free access to the **S.P.A.R.K. Framework Assessment™**, granting you the chance to see what obstacles and opportunities are in your journey.

- **Scan the QR code at the end of this chapter to take the S.P.A.R.K. Framework Assessment™ when you're ready!**

After all, we have all had moments when we have doubted ourselves, wondering if we are really cut out for the role we are in. Most of us have faced nights when the weight of personal, professional, and leadership responsibilities feels unbearable. We know the drain and strain that happens in board meetings, at kitchen tables, in side hustles, and during every sleepless season. We have felt the spark go out—but we need a way to find out how to maneuver through it.

In those moments, the **S.P.A.R.K. Framework Assessment™** provides a grounded, practical way to ask:

What's my best next step, based on who I am and what truly matters here?

In our work through the **S.P.A.R.K. Framework Assessment™** we will:

- Expose gaps in internal systems.
- Provide data-driven, human-centered solutions.
- Equip leaders, professionals, consultants, and organizations with actionable roadmaps.
- Deliver measurable, lasting transformation you can see and feel, not just rhetoric.

Why does that matter?

Because in today's workforce, retention is your revenue strategy. Internal systems that don't speak "human" will always fail the humans they're meant to serve. The **S.P.A.R.K. Framework Assessment™ Ecosystem** helps you build internal systems that finally speak your team's and your consumers' language—so that people want to stay, contribute, and grow with you.

That's what this framework makes possible. For many of us, this helps us seek to lead with deep human understanding while strategically integrating tools—including AI—that free us to focus on what only humans can do—innovate, empathize, inspire, and create meaningful change. We can leverage the **S.P.A.R.K. Framework Assessment™** to stop choosing between humanity and technology. Instead, we can serve the complex, multi-dimensional consumers and communities of today.

We get to rebuild, restructure, and humanize from the inside out—from rhetoric to results, from burnout to brilliance, from autopilot to aligned action. The **S.P.A.R.K. Framework™** is the framework that will guide you there.

Let's unpack how each pillar supports this mission and how it empowers you as a leader.

<u>S.P.A.R.K.</u>	<u>Focuses On:</u>	<u>Grants You a Way To:</u>
[S]trategy Pillar	Clarifying where you're going and *why*, aligned with who you are and the humans you serve.	Stop chasing every opportunity and start moving in one clear, values-aligned direction.
[P]lanning Pillar	Turning strategy into a realistic, human-centered roadmap (capacity, timing, resources, real life).	Stop living in crisis mode and start leading with intention, structure, and sustainable pacing.
[A]ction Pillar	Taking aligned, focused steps that match your strategy and values—not reactive busyness.	Stop confusing motion with progress and start doing the work that actually moves the needle.
[R]esults Pillar	Looking honestly at what's working and what isn't—personally, with your team, and in your systems.	Celebrate real wins, learn from misses without shame, and adjust quickly with clarity.
[K]PI Knowledge Pillar	Using data, metrics, and feedback as information—not identity—to guide decisions.	Measure what truly matters, so that numbers serve your humanity and mission, not the other way around.

To dive into how leaders like you are using the **S.P.A.R.K. Framework™**, I would like to introduce you to three individuals who have embodied this leadership model and created organizations that empowered each individual human within the company, all while reigniting their personal sense of purpose in their role.

Maria's Story: The Mother, Leader, and Human

Maria is a senior director at a Fortune 500 technology company. In her role, she achieved every metric her organization valued, hit her revenue targets, successfully led product launches, and earned regular recognition from her leadership. Yet, when she came home to her two young children each evening, she felt disconnected from who she wanted to be as both a leader and a mother.

"I used to wake up excited about the problems I could solve," Maria confessed. "Now, I wake up dreading the problems that will be thrown at me." At work, she operated on autopilot, simply going through the motions without feeling drive or satisfaction from the role. By day's end, she was exhausted and irritable. Each evening, she struggled to be present with her family; her mind was still trapped in endless corporate processes that consumed her.

Maria's experience is not unique. It is symptomatic of an organization still operating on outdated performance models that measured activity over impact, compliance over innovation. The company had sophisticated AI systems for data analysis, but these tools were layered onto old hierarchical structures that stifled creativity and human connection. Maria served consumers who valued authenticity and innovation yet worked within internal systems that were designed for a world that no longer existed. Thus, she faced a continual drain.

Transformation began when Maria stopped seeing change as "risky" and instead recognized that staying in this continuous loop she was stuck in was the actual threat to her career, her team's potential, and her ability to be who she wanted to be.

It was time for a change.

Using the **S.P.A.R.K. Framework Assessment™**, Maria began to systematically identify which organizational processes created barriers to meaningful work and authentic leadership.

Right at the start, she discovered that her company used a project approval system that required 17 different sign-offs. Each innovative idea became a bureaucratic marathon. Instead of accepting this process as "how things are done here," Maria streamlined the approval process to maintain quality control yet accelerate decision-making. She leveraged AI tools to automate routine project tracking. This freed up human capacity for strategic thinking and creative problem-solving.

Next, she began to say no to initiatives that didn't align with long-term impact. She restructured team meetings to focus on problem-solving rather than status reporting. Most importantly, she positioned AI as an ally in human-centered work, not a replacement for human judgment and creativity.

Within six months, not only did Maria's engagement soar, but her team's innovation metrics improved by 40%. Additionally, employee satisfaction scores reached an all-time high. On a personal level, Maria found herself energized rather than drained at the end of the day. This enabled her to be fully present with her children because her work was aligned with her values.

The ripple effect was remarkable. Soon, other departments began asking Maria to share her approaches, and senior leadership took notice. Maria proved that what feels uncomfortable—challenging established processes—isn't "risky" when it's grounded in clear strategy and authentic purpose.

Here's a quick S.P.A.R.K. snapshot of how the [S]trategy Pillar transformed Maria's leadership and her life.

	<u>What Was True for Maria</u>	<u>S.P.A.R.K. – Strategy Lens</u>
Obstacle	Maria was a high-performing senior director who hit every metric on paper, but felt disconnected, drained, and on autopilot at work—while also being emotionally unavailable at home. Her organization rewarded activity over impact and compliance over innovation, with outdated processes (like a 17-step approval system) that made meaningful work feel impossible.	[S]trategy was defined **for** Maria by legacy systems and surface metrics, instead of being defined **by** her values, purpose, and the humans she served.
Opportunity	Maria realized that the real "risk" wasn't pursuing change—it was remaining in the same repetitive cycle. She had an opportunity to realign her leadership with her original purpose (creating meaningful technological solutions) and to redesign internal processes allowing her team to achieve the work they were capable of.	Maria had the opportunity to ask strategic questions: *What truly matters here? Who are we serving? What kind of leader and mother do I want to be?* Strategy could become her anchor, not just the company's dashboard.
Our Strategic Approach	Using the **S.P.A.R.K. Framework™**, Maria started with **Strategy**. Maria clarified a human-centered strategic vision for herself and her team, then: 1) Identified which processes (like the 17 signoffs) were blocking that vision. 2) Designed a streamlined approval process that kept quality while removing unnecessary friction. 3) Repositioned AI as a tool to automate routine tracking, freeing humans for creativity and problem-solving. 4) Refocused meetings around real problem-solving instead of status updates.	[S]trategy meant **choosing aligned direction**: Saying no to misaligned initiatives, saying yes to what served long-term impact, and redesigning systems to reflect that choice. Her strategy became: *"We exist to create meaningful solutions—and our processes must serve that goal, versus sabotage it."*

	<u>What Was True for Maria</u>	<u>S.P.A.R.K. – Strategy Lens</u>
Outcome	Within six months, Maria's engagement and energy significantly increased, her team's innovation metrics improved by 40%, and employee satisfaction hit an all-time high. She came home more present with her children because her work was now aligned with her values. Other departments began asking her to share her approach, and senior leaders took notice.	[S]trategy moved Maria from **performing in a broken internal system** to **leading a human-centered one**. She proved that when strategy is grounded in purpose and people—not just metrics—both performance and well-being rise together.

Maria's story demonstrates what is possible when a leader courageously reclaims [S]trategy—aligning their work with personal values and redesigning internal systems to serve humans, not just metrics.

David's Story: The CEO, Father, and Community Leader

David's story reminds us that strategy doesn't live in theory; it must be carried out through real decisions, especially when the stakes are high. David is the CEO of a mid-sized manufacturing company. Several years into this role, he faced a crisis that tested everything he believed about leadership. When automation threatened 30% of his workforce, traditional leadership advice suggested quick layoffs and rapid technological adoption to maintain profit margins. His board pressured him, industry analysts watched, and competitors were making cuts to maintain the bottom line.

It seemed like everyone wanted to know—would David follow suit?

David, however, wasn't just a CEO. He was a father of three, a member of his local community, and someone who grew up in a blue-collar family where job security meant everything. His employees weren't just numbers on a spreadsheet. They were his neighbors, parents who coached his kids' soccer teams, and families he'd known for years.

Instead of reacting from fear, David stayed grounded in his company's foundational mission, vision and value: Our people are our greatest asset. He recognized that the "standard" approach of cutting staff to lower payroll wasn't just outdated, it was counterproductive in a world where adaptability and institutional knowledge are competitive advantages. He knew that treating people as disposable resources was designed for a predictable, static business environment that no longer existed.

What others called "risky"—investing in people during uncertainty—David understood as essential for sustainable success and authentic leadership. Using the **S.P.A.R.K. Framework™ Ecosystem**, he chose a different path. He invested in comprehensive retraining programs, created new roles that leveraged human creativity alongside automation, and transparently communicated the company's evolution to all stakeholders. This included maintaining open lines of communication with the families and community members who depended on their jobs.

Next, David selected AI vendors who shared his commitment to augment human work rather than eliminate it. Together, they used AI for predictive maintenance and quality control while training employees to interpret data insights and make strategic decisions. The transition took longer and required more upfront investment, but the results spoke for themselves: zero involuntary layoffs occurred. Conversely, David's employee base was able to increase productivity, improve employee loyalty, and forge a company culture that became a recruiting magnet in their industry.

Three years later, David's company outperformed competitors who had chosen the "quick fix" approach. More significantly, David's approach crafted an organization that was antifragile. It didn't just survive disruption; it grew stronger because of it. David could look his neighbors in the eye, knowing he had built something that honored both business success and human dignity. His leadership reflected the values he proudly was able to pass on to his children.

Let's unpack at how the **[P]**lanning Pillar within the **S.P.A.R.K. Framework Assessment™** shaped David's decisions when automation threatened 30% of his workforce. Here's a breakdown of his journey, from obstacle to opportunity, the options he chose, and the outcomes that followed.

	<u>**What Was True for David**</u>	<u>**S.P.A.R.K. – Planning Lens**</u>
Obstacle	As CEO of a mid-sized manufacturing company, David faced automation that threatened 30% of his workforce. The board and industry norms pushed for quick layoffs to protect margins. Employees at risk weren't abstract "FTEs"—they were neighbors, parents on his kids' teams, and families he knew.	The default **plan** handed to David was purely financial and fear based. It sought to "cut" people, protect profit, and move on quickly. Planning was seen as a spreadsheet exercise, versus one with a human, organizational, and community impact.
Opportunity	David recognized that the old playbook—treating people as disposable—was designed for a static world that no longer existed. He recognized an opportunity to design a path that honored his values, preserved institutional knowledge, and still embraced automation.	**[P]**lanning became the bridge between his **values** ("people are our greatest asset") and his **reality** (automation is coming either way). The question shifted from *"Who do we cut?"* to *"How do we bring our people with us?"*

	<u>What Was True for David</u>	<u>S.P.A.R.K. – Planning Lens</u>
Our Strategic Approach	Using the **S.P.A.R.K. Framework™**, David centered on [**P**]lanning, in which he: 1) Mapped which roles were at risk and what skills could transfer. 2) Designed retraining and upskilling pathways tied to upcoming automated processes. 3) Created new roles that combined human creativity and judgment with automated tools. 4) Partnered with AI vendors aligned with augmenting— not replacing—human work. 5) Built a transparent communication plan for employees, families, and community stakeholders.	[**P**]lanning shifted toward a **human-centered roadmap**. Each step, investment, and partnership was intentionally designed for people and technology to coexist and co-evolve. Planning turned disruption into a structured path forward instead of a chaotic reaction.
Outcome	The transition took longer and required more upfront investment, but it led to zero involuntary layoffs, increased productivity, stronger employee loyalty, and a culture that became a recruiting magnet. Three years later, the company outperformed competitors who chose quick layoffs. David could look his children and community members in the eye, knowing he honored both business success and human dignity.	[**P**]lanning transformed a potential mass layoff into a strategic, values-aligned evolution. David didn't just keep his company alive; he made it antifragile. The plan he chose demonstrated that planning isn't about controlling people—it's about designing a future where people and systems can thrive together.

David's story reveals what happens when a leader refuses to accept a default plan and instead uses [**P**]lanning to design a human-centered path through disruption. But even the most thoughtful strategy and planning mean nothing if they stay on paper. David knew that at some point, leaders must move from insight to implementation, from intention to courageous follow-through.

Sarah's Story: The Executive, Community Member, and Mission-Driven Leader

Sarah's story shows us how even the most thoughtful strategy and planning mean nothing if they stay on paper. She embodies what it means to move from insight to implementation, from intention to courageous follow-through.

As a nonprofit executive, Sarah was at a breaking point when her organization nearly collapsed during a leadership transition. Board members argued, funding was uncertain, staff morale was at an all-time low, and the community they served was losing trust. Sarah felt like she was failing everyone—not just professionally, but personally. As someone who had dedicated her life to service, watching the mission she deeply believed in crumbling felt like a betrayal of everything she stood for.

Sarah's initial response to organizational crisis and mission drift was to resign. She was convinced that her leadership was the problem, but there was more to it. Her situation perfectly illustrated how outdated nonprofit management approaches—governance structures designed in the 1950s, funding models that prioritized donor preferences over community needs, and communication systems that operated in silos—were actually the root cause of the crisis, not her leadership capabilities.

Sarah faced a choice: Do I continue trying to make broken internal systems work or embrace the discomfort of systematic transformation? What seemed like the risky path—overhauling established processes during a crisis—proved to be the only sustainable option for serving the authentic needs of her community.

Instead of abandoning her post, Sarah used the **S.P.A.R.K. Framework™** to rebuild from the ground up. She started with **[S]**trategy, examining which organizational structures and processes were actively undermining the mission. She discovered that their board meetings consumed hours on procedural discussions while spending minutes on programmatic impact. She found out that their fundraising approach was built around donor cultivation events that cost nearly as much as they raised.

These two discoveries led her to plan a new approach. She engaged in transparent **[P]**lanning sessions with board members and staff to create alignment around priorities.

Next, came **[A]**ction. Sarah integrated AI tools for donor management and impact measurement. This provided unprecedented visibility into program effectiveness while reducing administrative burden. She also took decisive **[A]**ction to address internal systemic issues that had been ignored for years.

To increase transparency and regain donor trust, she implemented **[R]**esults tracking that measured both programmatic impact and organizational health. She built the proper **[K]**PI Knowledge systems that ensured lessons learned would guide future decisions, ending the cycle of crisis leadership changes.

Eighteen months later, Sarah's nonprofit was thriving again. More importantly, it was sustainable. The organization had moved from crisis management to strategic leadership, from reactive funding to proactive resource development, and from siloed departments to integrated impact delivery. Staff retention improved, funding stabilized, and community impact reached new levels. Sarah didn't just save her organization; she transformed it into a model that other nonprofits began studying and replicating.

Personally, Sarah rediscovered her purpose and sense of meaning. She began to finally sleep at night, knowing that the organization was truly serving the community in a way that honored the mission and the people who made it possible.

	What Was True for Sarah	**S.P.A.R.K. – Action Lens**
Obstacle	As a nonprofit executive in the middle of a leadership transition, Sarah was surrounded by chaos. She faced a divided board, unstable funding, low staff morale, and a community who had lost trust. She internalized the crisis as a personal failure and considered resignation, though the root issue was outdated governance, siloed communication, and funding models that prioritized donors versus community needs.	Sarah was stuck in **defeatist action**—over-functioning emotionally while feeling powerless to change the system. Action meant constant firefighting, self-blame, and survival instead of intentional, mission-aligned decisions.
Opportunity	Sarah realized she had a choice: Keep pushing harder inside broken internal systems or embrace the discomfort of systemic change. What looked "risky" (overhauling structures in a crisis) was the only way to honor the mission and the people they served.	Overhauling structure created an opening for **aligned action**. This meant not just doing more but doing the *right* things. Action became rooted in mission, values, and long-term impact rather than fear and urgency.

	What Was True for Sarah	**S.P.A.R.K. – Action Lens**
Our Strategic Approach	Using the **S.P.A.R.K. Framework™**, Sarah moved from insight to **Action.** She: 1) Acted on **Strategy** by naming which structures undermined the mission (board agendas, fundraising models, etc.). 2) Led **Planning** sessions with her board and staff to align priorities and responsibilities. 3) Took courageous **Action** to redesign board meetings around impact, overhaul fundraising to reflect community needs, and implement AI tools for donor management and impact tracking. 4) Established **Results** metrics for both program impact and organizational health. 5) Built **Knowledge** systems so the organization could learn from this crisis instead of repeat it.	[A]ction meant taking **decisive, values-driven steps, which included**: staying in her role instead of resigning, confronting long-ignored systemic issues, and implementing new tools that aligned with their mission. Action turned reflection into concrete change.
Outcome	Within 18 months, the nonprofit moved from near-collapse to stability and growth. Staff retention improved, funding stabilized, community trust was rebuilt, and impact increased. The organization became a model other nonprofit leaders studied. Most importantly, Sarah could finally sleep at night, knowing the mission she loved was being carried out in a way that honored both the community and the people who did the work.	[A]ction transformed a crisis into a turning point. By taking aligned, courageous action instead of quitting or maintaining the status quo, Sarah didn't just save an organization, she reshaped it into a sustainable, mission-true, human-centered model of leadership.

This is what happens when you lead from your roots rather than your reactions.

Each of these leaders discovered that what others called "risky", challenging established processes, staying true to values under pressure, honoring the full scope of what makes us human—was crucial for sustainable success. They proved that when you're grounded in purpose you can address outdated processes, policy, and procedures for true transformation. They remind us that we don't just survive change—we have a chance to re-define our companies and shape our lives.

The consumers, employees, and communities we serve today are looking for more from us as leaders. As multi-dimensional humans, they expect leadership that reflects their complexity, not outdated mindsets and internal systems that reduce them to data points. This new model of leadership isn't a nice-to-have—it's a must-have for anyone who wants to build something that lasts and serves the world we live in.

Here's a quick snapshot of what happens when leaders and organizations *don't* embrace the "risk" of change and remain in a rut.

If You Don't Evolve Your Leadership…	What It Looks Like in Real Life	What the Data Shows
You lose your best talent	High performers quietly leave to join organizations that honor their whole selves, not just their output. The people needed most are the first to walk away.	Low employee engagement costs the global economy an estimated **US$8.9 trillion**, about **9% of global GDP** *(Gallup, 2024 State of the Global Workplace and AHTD)*.
You drain your people through burnout	Exhaustion, anxiety, and emotional fatigue become the norm. Sick days rise, "quiet quitting" spreads, and mental health issues threaten performance and retention.	Depression and anxiety are responsible for around **12 billion lost working days** each year, costing the global economy about **US$1 trillion** annually in lost productivity *(World Health Organization, International Labour Organization)*.
You lose your best customers	Customers and clients move toward brands that reflect their values and humanity. Loyalty erodes, and reputation lost damages buyer's trust.	**82%** of shoppers want a brand's values to align with their own, and about **75%** say they've parted ways with a brand over a conflict in values *(Harris Poll / Google Cloud study, Retail TouchPoints)*.
Your performance and market share erode	Innovation slows, silos grow, and teams spend more time managing dysfunction than creating value.	Organizations with ineffective leadership see close to a **29% reduction in productivity** and a **23% increase in turnover** *(Center for Creative Leadership, Afterburner)*.
Burnout spreads through your managers and teams	Managers carry impossible loads, become disengaged, and unintentionally pass that stress onto their teams. Culture becomes survival-focused, not purpose-driven.	Global research links poor working environments and leadership to large-scale productivity loss due to mental health challenges, reinforcing that burnout is a systemic leadership issue—not an individual weakness

If You Don't Evolve Your Leadership…	What It Looks Like in Real Life	What the Data Shows
		(World Health Organization, International Labour Organization).
Innovation and creativity flatline	People stop speaking up, taking risks, or offering bold ideas. Everyone plays it safe, and the organization slowly stagnates.	Studies show that **inclusive, psychologically safe leadership** is positively related to innovative performance, voice, and creative behavior at work *(various inclusive leadership and psychological safety meta-analyses).*
You underinvest in leadership and pay for it later	Leadership stays reactive and transactional. You "save" money on development but quietly spend it on turnover, rework, and lost opportunities.	Companies with strong leadership development programs are nearly **2.4 times more likely** to hit their performance targets and enjoy significantly better financial outcomes *(McKinsey, Culture Partners, other leadership ROI studies).*
You risk losing your highest-potential people	Emerging leaders don't see a path for growth, so they mentally and physically check out—often taking their talent elsewhere.	Younger high-potential employees are **2.4 times more likely to stay** when organizations provide meaningful leadership development and growth experiences *(DDI, ATD).*

However, when you embrace **grounded, human-centered leadership**—leading from a steady, values-rooted center rather than fear, urgency, or performance pressure—the story changes completely.

When You Embrace Grounded, Human-Centered Leadership…	What It Looks Like in Real Life	What It Sets You Up For (S.P.A.R.K. Lens)
You become the leader everyone wants to work for and with.	People seek you out as a mentor, advocate, and thought partner. Your team feels safe sharing ideas, feedback, and honest concerns.	**Strategy & Action:** You demonstrate clear, human-centered direction and courageous follow-through that builds trust, not fear.
You build organizations that attract and retain top talent because people thrive when they're seen and valued as	Engagement rises, turnover drops, and your culture becomes a magnet for high-caliber, values-aligned people.	**Planning & Results:** You design internal systems that support well-being and growth, while measuring what metrics drive retention and performance.

When You Embrace Grounded, Human-Centered Leadership...	What It Looks Like in Real Life	What It Sets You Up For (S.P.A.R.K. Lens)
whole humans.		
You create customer loyalty that transcends price competition because your brand represents authentic values.	Customers stay, refer others, and forgive mistakes because they believe in who you are and what you stand for.	**Strategy & KPI Knowledge:** You align your brand, decisions, and metrics with genuine human needs and values, not just short-term gains.
You develop resilience that allows you to navigate any disruption because your foundation is unshakeable.	Disruptions still come, but you and your team respond with clarity instead of panic. You adapt without losing who you are.	**Planning & Action:** You build flexible plans and take aligned steps that keep your purpose and people at the forefront during change.
You achieve sustainable success that doesn't require you to sacrifice your personal life, health, or integrity.	You meet goals without burning out. Your relationships, well-being, and sense of self stay intact as you continuously develop.	**Strategy, Planning, Action, Results, and KPI Knowledge** You embody a human-centered leadership model for long-term, holistic success.

Grounded leadership isn't a trendy label, it's the kind of leader you become when your values, your behavior, and your internal systems all tell the same story and are the core of the grounded leadership being rooted.

To be rooted as a leader means you know what you stand for.

Your identity isn't determined by your latest performance review, your title, or the mood of the boardroom. You have the opportunity to choose a path that allows you to be anchored in your values, purpose, faith, and deep conviction about the kind of impact you want to make.

Storms will come, but there is a way to keep you from being yanked around by every crisis, trend, or opinion. This makes you a grounded and rooted leader who in turn respects your team members' values, not just their output. You see the **whole human** in front of you—the parent, the coach, the young student and professional, the caregiver, the dreamer, the culture carrier—not just the role they fill on an org chart. You pay it forward as you engage authentically, not performatively. You listen, you ask real questions, you tell the truth even when it's uncomfortable, and you invite your team to do the same.

Grounded leaders create environments where people don't have to shrink themselves to fit in. Your team knows where you stand and what you stand for. They trust that you'll hold a high standard *and* hold space for their well-being. You move with urgency when needed, but you don't let urgency dictate your identity, your integrity, strategies or your impact. Your roots decide that, not the pressure of the moment or circumstance. That's the leader this book is calling you to become—title or no title. Rooted, honest, and human. Someone who can carry compassion, clarity, and soul.

This is where we shift—from naming the problem to living the solution.

REFLECTION QUESTIONS

Take a few moments to ground yourself and reflect on where you are right now, both personally and professionally. These questions are designed to help you connect more deeply with the journey ahead:

What does "being grounded" mean to me right now?

____

____

In what areas of my life or leadership have I been operating on autopilot?

____

____

What values do I want to anchor into as I grow?

____

____

When was the last time I felt truly aligned with both my purpose and my pace?

____

____

What is one belief I'm ready to release and one I'm ready to reclaim?

____

____

How do I define success for myself? Does that definition reflect my truth or someone else's?

Write your responses in the space above or in a journal. Return to them often as you work through the **S.P.A.R.K. Framework™**.

Quote to Close the Chapter:

You don't have to reset. You have to go deeper and restructure at the root.

— Dr. Michelle Brown

SCAN TO TAKE The S.P.A.R.K. Framework **Assessment™**

Next Up: Chapter 2 – Find Your S.P.A.R.K.: Activating Your Rise

In this next chapter, we'll uncover what's been keeping you stuck in outdated internal systems and mindsets of comfort and ignite the inner **S.P.A.R.K.** that will carry you, your teams, and organization into your next level of leadership to redefine the leaders now and the future. This is where sustainable transformation begins, not with what happened to you in the past or your current environment, but with what you choose to do next with that information and use it to move forward, faster, together toward solutions.

We are discussing solutions in this book and going from rhetoric to results with our solution-focused **S.P.A.R.K. Framework Assessment™ and Ecosystem.**

Let's activate your rise in the next chapter!

CHAPTER 2 – IGNITING YOUR S.P.A.R.K
ACTIVATING YOUR RISE

In Chapter 1, we established the fact around how the future belongs to leaders who can integrate human-centered approaches with technological advancement. Such exceptional leaders refuse to fragment themselves to fit outdated models and instead provide the experience their teams and customers need, without losing a competitive edge. This balance meets our consumers, employees, and communities we serve exactly as they are—multi-dimensional humans who expect us to reflect their complexity.

To put this into action, we must get personal.

Let's get something straight—great leadership isn't about just embracing hardship or making it through hard times. Most of us have faced struggle. Yet powering through is not what makes us credible. What makes us powerful leaders is *how* we use those experiences to shape our decisions, build our confidence, and direct ours and our teams' growth. Your challenges don't define you, but they do train you. They teach you what to tolerate, what to pursue, what to release, and what to reclaim. But here's what traditional, self-development thought leaders won't tell you: Your past experiences aren't just personal growth material—they're a bedrock of organizational intelligence. The challenges you've overcome in your individual journey are the same patterns that need transformation in the internal systems around you. The belief systems that previously limited your potential are also hiding in our workplaces and corporate hallways. Many times, these limiting frameworks are choking the life out of teams, departments, and entire industries then trickle into our daily personal lives.

Every time you embrace personal transformation, that choice has a chance to move beyond you and become a systemic revolution. When you refuse to accept outdated approaches in your own life, you become a catalyst for updating broken internal systems everywhere you go. It starts quietly. This reform begins the moment you stop agreeing to "how we've always done it" when those methods are clearly draining people. It builds every time you question policies, meeting rhythms, and unspoken rules that require you, or your team, to fragment yourselves to fit in. It expands when you set new boundaries around your time, values, and wellbeing. This revolution takes hold when these new practices ripple outward into organizational culture as you lead your team to take the same steps you have just modeled for them.

Over time, the action steps we take force the internal system to respond. Workflows are redesigned, priorities get clarified, and metrics are refined to measure what truly matters versus what's just easy to count. Other people begin to take similar action now that they can see that there is, in fact, another way to lead and live authentically. Therefore, your steps of courage move beyond an individual rise. Instead, you also redefine how others work, lead, and create together—one decision, one conversation, one internal system at a time.

How personal transformation rewrites internal systems around you:

When You Refuse Outdated Approaches In Your Own Life…	What You Actually Do	How It Starts Changing the Internal System
You reject the belief that constant availability equals value.	You stop replying to emails at all hours, set clear communication boundaries, and tell your team you don't expect 24/7 responses.	The unspoken rule that "if you're not always on, you're not committed" begins to break. Expectations reset, burnout decreases, and a healthier pace is normalized.
You stop wasting time on performative meetings.	You push back on a recurring 90-minute status meeting and turn it into a focused written update, using live time for problem-solving and connection.	The team starts to prioritize purpose-driven gatherings over draining meetings. Productivity rises and people believe their time is respected.
You refuse to define performance by output alone.	You question why performance reviews only reward numbers and advocate for including collaboration, growth, and well-being in evaluations.	Metrics evolve to measure stated values. The organization slowly shifts from "do more" to "grow well," shaping promotions, rewards, and culture.
You ensure that technology will not be used to dehumanize work.	You insist AI and tech tools are used to remove busy work and support human creativity, not as an excuse to demand faster output harder or cut people out.	Tech is reframed as a partner, not a threat. Internal systems are redesigned to amplify human strengths, not replace them. In turn, this changes how decisions about tools and staffing are made.

Our commitment to transform ourselves goes beyond our individual rise. Instead, it opens up crucial conversations which challenge how we work, lead, and create together.

The **S.P.A.R.K. Framework™** sits on a foundation of our deeply personal stories of transformation. It is always rooted from our lived experiences, deep reflection, and the need for something authentic to bridge healing and high performance just like our personal and professional journeys. It recognizes that we can't separate individual transformation from organizational evolution. The same outdated thinking patterns that keep individuals stuck are the same patterns that create toxic work cultures, inefficient processes, and unsustainable business models.

Before I was a business owner, strategist, or leader, I was an angry, disconnected, and disruptive teenage girl. One year before entering 9th grade, after being in yet another fight, I found myself in the principal's office facing expulsion. Two teachers looked at me and asked one simple, soul-stirring question: "Is this how you want to be remembered?"

What those teachers didn't realize the day they pulled me aside and challenged my actions was that they were modeling what transformational leadership looks like. Instead of simply punishing disruptive behavior—the traditional disciplinary approach—they helped me see that I had the power to rewrite my story. They didn't address my actions and leave it there; they addressed the internal patterns of beliefs I held that created those actions.

I didn't know how one single question would change the trajectory of my life. In that moment, I didn't answer them. I stayed silent, baffled at how to respond, but something shifted inside me. That pause gave me space. And in that space, I made a decision. I didn't know exactly how to change, but I knew I would. I didn't ask for a detailed map or an elaborate path. I just started by letting their words ring in my mind and remind me that I could be more than I had become. I chose to rewrite my story—and followed it up with the right choices.

I turned D's and F's into straight A's. I became class president. I earned a full D-1 athletic scholarship. I didn't become a different person—I became a grounded one, someone who was unafraid to rise above where I had been. Through the process, I learned something crucial. Life doesn't change until you embrace change and act differently.

———————

My decision to stop limiting myself—to commit to improvement—and my willingness to measure what matters became more than personal development strategies. Eventually, they became transformation imperatives for each organization I walked into. **And that same power lives in you!**

Whether you're a corporate leader facing cultural barriers, teams and organizational challenges, a coach scaling your business, or a team member navigating leadership transition, this **S.P.A.R.K.** is already within you, waiting to ignite!

Let me remind you. Your **S.P.A.R.K.** isn't something you have to look outward to find—it's already within you, carved into your story, marked by every obstacle you have already overcome. From here, the framework simply gives structure, language, and a roadmap to what's inside you. It provides space for your personal decisions to move from internal to external as they start reshaping the environment around you.

Your decision to stop accepting limiting patterns is where **[S]**trategy begins.

Your commitment to systematic improvement is where **[P]**lanning and **[A]**ction come alive.

Your willingness to measure what truly matters is where **[R]**esults and **[K]**PI Knowledge redefine success.

How S.P.A.R.K. Turns Your Choices Into Systemic Change

<u>Your Choice as a Leader</u>	<u>How the S.P.A.R.K. Framework™ Helps</u>	<u>What This Looks Like in Practice</u>
You decide to stop accepting limiting patterns.	**[S]**trategy helps you clarify what you will no longer tolerate and what you're moving toward instead. It is based on your values and the humans you serve.	You name outdated norms ("we reward burnout," "we never say no to clients") and replace them with a clear, human-centered strategic direction your team can align with.
You commit to systematic improvement, not one-off fixes.	**[P]**lanning and **[A]**ction turn your intention into a roadmap. They form concrete steps that rebuild internal systems from the inside out.	You redesign meeting rhythms, workflows, and decision paths. You pilot new processes, gather feedback, and keep iterating instead of slipping back into "how it's always been."
You're willing to measure what matters.	**[R]**esults and **[K]**PI Knowledge shift what you track and celebrate, allowing your metrics to reflect real impact versus busyness.	You expand success measures to include engagement, retention, well-being, innovation, and values alignment—not just revenue or output. This data is used to make wiser decisions.
You choose to lead as a whole human, not as a title.	The whole **S.P.A.R.K. Framework™ Ecosystem** keeps your leadership integrated—aligning your inner world (purpose, values, mindset) with your outer world (systems, processes, metrics).	Whether your role is at the top or bottom of an org chart, you show up consistently as yourself. The spaces you lead are more human, more effective, and more resilient.

Your individual breakthrough is a blueprint for internal systems change. Your current reality may not match your vision yet, but one decision can shift everything. That decision is more than personal—it's professional, organizational, and cultural. Every time you decide to stop accepting outdated approaches, practices, processes, policies and procedures in your own growth, you simultaneously decide to stop enabling outdated internal systems in your personal and professional environments.

Consider Marcus, a mid-level manager at a healthcare organization. Marcus felt trapped in endless committee meetings, which produced reports no one read. For years, it seemed everyone collectively decided to accept this as "corporate culture," and coped with the inefficiency. But Marcus recognized that his frustration wasn't a personal problem—it was an internal systems problem that affected patient care, staff morale, and organizational effectiveness.

Marcus did more than change his personal approach to meetings—he transformed how his department approached collaborative decision-making. **[S]**trategy helped identify exactly which internal systems were sabotaging their efforts to provide excellent patient care. He was then able to identify which meetings were actually necessary versus which ones were organizational habits. **[P]**lanning allowed for designed and streamlined communication protocols. **[A]**ction meant implementing pilot programs. **[R]**esults tracking indicated where improvements happened in both decision speed and implementation quality. **[K]**PI Knowledge sharing moved these improvements into other departments, removed any duplicate effort, and provided valuable insight for decision making, not just tracking.

Within eight months, Marcus's department reduced meeting time by 60%. They also increased project completion rates by 35%. More importantly, staff satisfaction increased as employees felt their time was respected and their contributions made a real impact. Marcus proved his personal frustration with outdated internal systems had power to become a catalyst for systematic improvement.

Just like Marcus, you don't have to wait for permission to ignite your spark. You don't need to hit rock bottom. Instead, as you feel a gnawing internal frustration you simply must be willing to choose differently and decide who you're becoming and what you will do next. The discomfort you feel when working within broken internal systems and processes isn't a signal that you need to adapt better; it's intelligence telling you that those internal systems and processes need to evolve. As you follow through on your choice to move beyond inefficient internal systems, you get to model what's possible for everyone around you. You prove that outdated internal systems don't have to be permanent. In the end, you have a chance to discover that your impatience with outdated approaches was not an unprofessional mindset, it was strategic wisdom. From here, you have upgraded the experience for everyone who comes after you.

The beauty of the **S.P.A.R.K. Framework™ Ecosystem** is that it works at every level. Whether you are entry level, a team leader, the department head, or have a role in the C-Suite—you are a part of building organizational culture. We each have a chance to create transformation that bridges personal development and professional excellence, individual growth, and collective impact.

Let's dive into scenarios that showcase how we can use the **S.P.A.R.K. Framework™** based on where we sit in an organization.

For Leadership Teams:

Scenario: A leadership team is struggling with low morale, high turnover, and unclear direction. Instead of launching another "team-building initiative," they pause to reflect on why these issues persist. The traditional approach they have used for years has been to schedule a company retreat or design a new mission statement, complete with fresh posters for the hallways. However, this leadership recognizes the fact that low morale and high turnover are symptoms of deeper issues.

They realize that what feels "risky"—questioning current established approaches and organizational structures—is actually the safest path forward. They perceive that the greater risk they are facing is a continuation of losing talent and organizational momentum while competitors are evolving.

To face this challenge, they choose to go deeper. They ignite their spark by committing to realign their leadership culture using the **S.P.A.R.K. Framework Assessment™** pillars.

Using **[S]**trategy, they examined which leadership practices and structures have created barriers to employee engagement. They discovered that their current performance review system, designed in the 1990s, focuses on individual achievement rather than collaborative impact. Their communication flows were hierarchical, yet their work requires cross-functional innovation.

Using **[P]**lanning, they designed an approach that integrates emotional intelligence with technical expertise. They built a performance evaluation system that measures both results and relationship quality. Lastly, they created communication protocols that match their collaborative work style.

Using **[A]**ction, they implemented these changes gradually, starting with pilot teams. They measured impact and adjusted based on feedback. They used AI tools to track engagement patterns and identify early warning signs of disengagement. Throughout this change, human touch remained central to all leadership development.

Using **[R]**esults, they tracked measures beyond traditional HR numbers such as retention and satisfaction. They also measured innovation output, cross-departmental collaboration, and employee growth trajectories. They discovered that departments that had the most effective leadership development showed 40% higher innovation rates.

Using **[K]**PI Knowledge systems, they ensured that each leadership lesson learned was captured, shared, and integrated into ongoing development versus something lost during leadership transitions.

The result?

With the **S.P.A.R.K. Framework™ Ecosystem** in place, each team then moves from reactive management to purpose-driven leadership. The organization as a whole was able to have clear strategic goals, improve internal communication, and align leadership behavior with core values. Most importantly, senior leadership proved that what seemed like "risky" changes created the stability and sustainability every person in the company was seeking all along.

This S.P.A.R.K. Snapshot™ breaks down how this leadership team was able to lead their shift—and how you can start doing the same in your own organization:

S.P.A.R.K. Pillar	How They Used It:	How Your Team Can Begin:
[S]trategy	Leadership stopped treating low morale and turnover as "people problems" and named them as **internal system problems** driven by outdated performance reviews and rigid communication structures.	**Ask:** "If this isn't just a people issue, what system, habit, or structure is feeding it?" Define 1–2 likely culprits (e.g. performance reviews, communication norms, workload expectations).
[P]lanning	Leadership chose specific systems to redesign, starting with performance reviews and leadership communication. They mapped a clear "old way → new way" path which aligned with their values and collaboration needs.	Pick **one** internal system to improve first. Sketch a simple "Old Way → New Way" that better supports collaboration, clarity, and humans—versus output alone.
[A]ction	Leadership piloted the new approaches with select teams, communicated openly about the changes, gathered feedback, and adjusted instead of forcing a massive rollout.	**Start small.** Test your "New Way" with one team or project. Invite honest feedback and adjust as you go, rather than aiming for perfection on Day One.
[R]esults	Leadership measured more than standard HR numbers such as retention. Instead, they measured engagement, cross-team collaboration, and innovation. They noticed innovation rose in teams with stronger leadership development.	Decide 3–4 things to measure beyond output (e.g., engagement, collaboration, ideas implemented, internal mobility, etc.). Review these regularly with your team.
[K]PI Knowledge	Leadership documented what had favorable results, captured leadership lessons learned, and built those insights into ongoing development, ensuring progress would not be lost during future transitions.	Write down what you have learned, what you changed, and why. Turn wins into simple, repeatable practices so the learning outlives any one leader or season.

Reflection:

Which outdated internal system is your organization reacting to versus leading?

____

____

Which S.P.A.R.K. Framework™ Pillar can you use to ignite clarity in that one area?

____

____

When organizations shift their internal systems, everything changes—including communication, culture, retention, innovation, and return on investment. Keep in mind, however, that none of these internal systems move on their own. They change because **leaders choose to see, decide,** and **lead differently**.

Behind every policy, meeting, performance review, or "ways we've always done it" is a human that makes a choice. Many times, that decision is made under pressure while that person carries their own invisible weight. That's why transformation does not happen at the organizational level alone. It must also land in the hearts, minds, and daily habits of the people who lead the work.

For that reason, we're going to zoom in from the organizational lens to the **leader** themselves as we move into the next scenario. Together, we will unpack how the **S.P.A.R.K. Framework™** helps a single leader move from overwhelm or misalignment to grounded clarity that creates the starting point for healthier teams, organizational cultures, and outcomes.

For Leaders:

In this **S.P.A.R.K. Framework™** snapshot, we see how one leader used the framework to move from burnout to grounded clarity—and how you can do the same. Below are more scenarios to dive into.

Scenario: Frederick, a senior manager, has felt overwhelmed and disconnected from the organization's mission. Rather than resign or check out, he pauses to revisit his personal "why."

This scenario reflects a common crisis point for leaders who feel as if traditional leadership development focuses on skill-building and goal-setting yet rarely addresses burnout. The typical approach is to challenge that leader to push forward, work longer hours, or seek another role. Yet these methods only treat the symptoms versus address the cause. However, Fredrick has recognized that his overwhelm isn't a personal failure—it's feedback. His burnout is an indicator informing him there is a misalignment between his values and his work environment. What appears on the surface to be a personal crisis is something deeper. It is an opportunity for internal system realignment and restructure.

S.P.A.R.K. Framework™ Shift:

Using the **S.P.A.R.K. Framework™**, Fredrick opted to map out a renewed leadership vision—anchored in clarity, intention, and legacy—and transform his stress into strategic direction.

Using **[S]**trategy, Frederick examined which aspects of his current role aligned with his core values, and which aspects drained his energy unnecessarily. He discovered that 60% of his time was spent on administrative tasks that could be streamlined or automated. Only 20% was spent on the strategic work that originally drew him to his current leadership role.

Using **[P]**lanning, Frederick redesigned his role to maximize impact while minimizing energy drain. This involved delegating more effectively, automating routine decisions, and restructuring team interactions to focus on high-value activities.

Using **[A]**ction, Frederick hosted honest conversations with his supervisor about his role expectations, what it looked like to implement new productivity systems, and what boundaries he needed to utilize in order to protect his capacity for strategic thinking. With his leadership on board, he then integrated AI tools for project management and data analysis. This preserved his time, which he allotted to relationship-building and creative problem-solving.

Using **[R]**esults tracking, Fredrick measured both professional outcomes and personal satisfaction metrics. He discovered that working fewer hours while focusing on aligned activities improved his leadership effectiveness and his team's performance.

Using **[K]**PI Knowledge, Frederick gathered regular reflection and feedback. This helped him to continuously refine his approach and model sustainable leadership for his team.

S.P.A.R.K. Pillar	How Fredrick Used It:	How You Can Begin:
[S]trategy	Fredrick paused before quitting and revisited his personal "why." He examined which parts of his role aligned with his core values and what drained him. Fredrick realized that 60% of his time was spent in admin work, while only 20% went toward the strategic work that once energized him.	List your main weekly activities. Mark each as value **Aligning** (energizing, meaningful) or **Draining** (misaligned, heavy). Notice where your time is spent vs. where you *want* it to go.
[P]lanning	Fredrick began systematically redesigning his role to maximize impact and minimize energy drain—delegating, streamlining, and restructuring how his team worked alongside him.	Choose **one** area to redesign (admin tasks, meetings, approvals, etc.). Create a simple plan. **Ask:** What can be delegated, automated, or dropped?
[A]ction	Fredrick took courageous action. He had honest conversations with his supervisor, set new boundaries, implemented productivity systems, and integrated AI to handle routine tasks. These changes allowed him to focus on strategic thinking and relationships.	Identify **one conversation** you need to have (about focus, expectations, boundaries, etc.) and **one small action** you can take this week to protect your time and position you for your most meaningful work.
[R]esults	Fredrick tracked not only performance outcomes, but also his personal satisfaction and energy. He discovered that working fewer hours on aligned activities improved team performance and his own effectiveness.	Decide 2–3 things to measure. For example: "hours spent on strategic work," "energy at the end of the day," or "team clarity." Check-in on these metrics weekly.
[K]PI Knowledge	Through regular reflection and feedback, Fredrick refined his approach. He began to model sustainable leadership for his team and turned his experience into shared wisdom, not just a private crisis averted.	Set a recurring check-in (weekly or monthly) to ask: **What's working?** **What's not?** **What needs to shift?** Capture insights ensuring you don't repeat a cycle of burnout.

Reflection:

What part of your leadership feels misaligned right now?

____

____

What would it look like to shift away from that and towards grounded clarity?

____

____

When you lead from grounded clarity, everything around you changes. Your team feels the difference. Your decisions carry greater conviction. Your leadership is less about holding it all together and more about modeling what wholeness looks like in real time.

But what if you have a role that does not require you to lead a team of direct reports, yet still requires great leadership skills? After all, many of today's leaders aren't only leading from within an organizational chart. Many lead as **service providers, facilitators, speakers, coaches and consultants**. These individuals hold space for others to experience transformation while actively seeking to manage their own. These professionals are the ones who build businesses, carry client expectations, and navigate the pressure to "scale"—all without losing their purpose.

The same **S.P.A.R.K. Framework™** principles apply for these leaders as well.

In the next scenario, we'll look at how coaches, consultants, and entrepreneurs can leverage the **S.P.A.R.K. Framework™ Ecosystem** to move from a scattered, survival-based hustle to a focused, sustainable business that honors their humanity and impact at the same time.

For Coaches and Consultants:

Here's a simple S.P.A.R.K. snapshot of how this consultant used the framework to move from scattered survival to structured success—and how you can start doing the same.

Scenario: Megan, a sales consultant, is stuck in a cycle of overwhelm and inconsistent outcomes. Her messaging is scattered. Her calendar is filled with draining commitments.

This is not an uncommon scenario. Many service providers feel trapped in the outdated belief that scaling means saying yes to everything. Megan is not the only one who has felt like she had to be "everything to everyone." Traditional business advice tells someone like Megan to diversify her offerings in order to maximize revenue. Yet this scattered approach undermines her expertise and creates an unsustainable workload.

Megan has recognized that her "safe" strategy—of accepting every opportunity to maintain cash flow—has created long-term instability for her business along with her own sense of professional dissatisfaction.

S.P.A.R.K. Framework™ Shift:

By using the **S.P.A.R.K. Framework™**, Megan defined her niche, implemented the right internal systems, and built strategic offers that reflected her strengths. She shifted from survival mode to structured success.

[S]trategy led Megan to identify her unique value proposition and ideal client profile based on her authentic expertise and passion, not market trends or competitor analysis. She realized that her background in organizational change management is her differentiator. This sets her apart from offering generic business coaching.

[P]lanning meant Megan had to transition away from scattered service offerings and move towards a focused area of expertise. This required her to complete current commitments and decline new projects that did not align with her specialized focus.

[A]ction required Megan to redesign her service delivery to leverage her expertise while using AI tools for client onboarding, progress tracking, and administrative tasks. She developed signature methodologies that could be replicated and scaled without losing quality or personal attention.

[R]esults tracking allowed Megan to measure both financial outcomes and her personal, professional satisfaction. She discovered that focusing on fewer, higher-value clients increased both revenue and impact while dramatically reducing her stress.

[K]PI Knowledge systems captured Megan's success and refined her methodology continuously, creating intellectual property that differentiated her practice in the marketplace.

S.P.A.R.K. Pillar	How Megan Used It:	How You Can Begin:
[S]trategy	Megan stopped trying to be "everything to everyone" and identified her unique value proposition and ideal client profile instead. She let her expertise—organizational change management—root her rather than chase every market trend.	**Ask yourself:** What am I truly best at, and who gets the most transformation from working with me? Write your offer statement: "I help [who] with [what] so they can [result]."
[P]lanning	Megan created a plan to transition from scattered services to a focused niche. She finished her current commitments and said no to new projects that didn't fit her specialization.	List your current offers and mark each: **Keep**, **Transition**, or **Release**. Create a simple 60–90-day plan to move toward one clear, focused expertise area.
[A]ction	Megan redesigned her services and delivery model, leveraged AI for onboarding/admin/client tracking, and built signature methodologies that could scale without reducing quality.	**Choose one action:** Streamline your onboarding, refine one signature offer, or document your core process into clear steps. Let AI handle tasks that don't need your brain or heart.
[R]esults	Megan tracked both financial outcomes and professional satisfaction. Fewer, better aligned clients led to higher revenue, deeper impact, and less stress.	**Decide 2–3 metrics to track.** For example: Ideal clients booked, average revenue per client, weekly energy level, etc. Review these numbers monthly to see what produces favorable results.
[K]PI Knowledge	Megan documented client transformation patterns, refined her frameworks, and turned her experience into proprietary intellectual property that differentiated her in the market.	Start capturing patterns. **Ask:** What do your best clients have in common? What steps do you repeat every time? Write each result and use it to shape your own method or framework.

Reflection Prompt:

Where have you traded impact for busyness?

____

____

What's your next aligned, strategic move that will allow you to reflect your true purpose?

____

____

The **S.P.A.R.K. Framework™** reshapes how entrepreneurs, coaches, and consultants move from scattered survival to structured, values-aligned success, but no matter your role, at the core you are a **human.**

Titles change. Seasons change. Business models change. But you carry _you_ into all of it—the caregiver, the partner, the friend, the community member, the dreamer who exists beyond any brand or bio. If we only apply the **S.P.A.R.K. Framework™** to what you do and never to who you are, we remain at the surface of the framework.

That's why in the next scenario, we're going to zoom out and discover how the **S.P.A.R.K. Framework™** applies to your whole life, not just your work. It is important to me that you have a chance to rise as an integrated, holistic human—no matter what title you hold or don't hold.

For so long, many of us have been taught that it is "professional" to split ourselves in two. On the other hand, the person we are at home should be and still is the person we are at work. We have been told to leave our feelings, our caregiving realities, our identities—and sometimes even our convictions—at the door in order to fit a mold that separates us from the full spectrum of who we are as a human.

But you are not two different people. You are one whole being who carries the same heart, history, responsibilities, and dreams into every space you enter. It does not matter if that is a boardroom, classroom, athletic field, hospital floor, kitchen, or a Teams or Zoom® room. The outdated mindset that demands we must compartmentalize our life in order to succeed is exactly what pushes so many high-capacity humans into burnout, identity confusion, and quiet resentment or quitting.

This is why the **S.P.A.R.K. Framework™** doesn't just apply to job titles or organizational charts—it applies to **you** as a whole person. It provides you with a way to reconnect your work with your values, your ambition with your wellbeing, and your responsibilities with your reality. Instead of asking you to choose between your career and your caregiving demands, your purpose or your peace, it helps you to design a life where each part can coexist and co-evolve, in what we call **CoEvolution™**.

For Individuals:

Let's unpack a simple **S.P.A.R.K. Framework™** snapshot, which defines how we can honor our whole self—not just our role or title—and what you can do to create similar change in your own life:

Scenario: Jeff feels like he is juggling a lot all at once. His work responsibilities plus caregiving for his child, and being present for his aging father, all while showing up for his friends, community and managing a household is becoming too much for him to handle. On top of it, he knows he should be caring for his own mind and body and remember who he is outside of what everyone needs from him. Some days he is hired to lead a team or a project. Other days he is brought in to help guide a family, classroom, group chat, small business, ministry, or community initiatives on how to thrive as he teaches one of his coaching workshops. From the outside, he looks "strong" and "responsible." On the inside, he feels stretched thin, behind on everything, and quietly unsure of who he is becoming. He constantly navigates the tension between who he wants to be and who everyone expects him to be.

This scenario represents the collision between responsibility and modern realities. Old frameworks assumed a linear path ("climb the ladder," "pick one lane"). They assume there is a clean separation between work and home life. Old models use a version of success that rarely accounts for caregiving, mental health, multiple callings, or identity shifts. But today, many of us are navigating layered, interconnected roles that don't fit into neat boxes or the traditional 9-5 thinking.

What feels overwhelming isn't a personal failure; it's the natural result of trying to keep us in line with outdated mindsets and internal beliefs that require us to manage our lives, which are far more complex, relational, and fast-moving than those models allow for. Jeff is overwhelmed, yet he wonders if one-dimensional career advice was ever built for the reality he faces as a multi-dimensional human.

S.P.A.R.K. Framework™ Shift:

Using the **S.P.A.R.K. Framework™**, Jeff decided to reconnect with his personal values and redefine what success means in this season of his life. He chose to set priorities that nurtured his well-being, daily duties, relationships, and deeper ambitions—all while allowing him to lead himself and others from a place of wholeness, not depletion.

[S]trategy meant Jeff had to get honest about which expectations he had in mind for himself that were truly his—and which ones he inherited from culture, family, work, or social media. He began to notice where his picture of "success" has been shaped by external validation more than by internal fulfillment. Instead of asking, *"What do people expect from me?"* he started asking, *"What matters most to me in this season of my life?"*

[P]lanning allowed Jeff to create an integrated approach to his life. This went beyond a "work plan" over here and a "personal life" over there. He started to design rhythms, routines, and support systems that honored his responsibilities (at home, at work, in the community) *and* his need for rest, joy, and growth. Instead of treating his roles as competing priorities, his plan let them coexist and support one another.

[A]ction meant Jeff made courageous, uncomfortable choices about where his time, energy, and attention would be spent. He started to say no to commitments that drained him without adding real value, and yes to what aligned with his values and capacity. He set boundaries with people, projects, and even his own habits. He allowed tools—including AI—to carry some of the mental load (reminders, planning, information) so his human energy could be spent on connection, creativity, and care.

[R]esults tracking meant Jeff could measure his **whole** life, not just his output. He was able to pay attention to his energy, emotions, relationships, and sense of purpose alongside the goals he was hitting. Over time, he noticed that when his choices lined up with his authentic values, both his inner peace *and* his outer impact were able to rise. He was not just doing more—he became more of who he was born to be.

[K]PI Knowledge internal systems let Jeff use simple, consistent reflection practices that kept him from slipping back into autopilot. He used different methods. Sometimes it was a weekly check-in, a journal prompt, or a quiet walk where he asked himself: *"What's working? What's not? What do I need now?"* He began to treat his life like a living system that could be adjusted with wisdom and compassion. He took what he learned and used it to lead others with similar care and compassion—no matter if that was at home, at work, or in his community.

S.P.A.R.K. Pillar	How Jeff Used It	How You Can Begin
[S]trategy	Jeff got honest about what expectations were versus what came from family, culture, work, or social media. He realized his version of "success" was based on external approval instead of his personal values.	Ask yourself: **"What matters most to me in this season of my life?"** List 3 values you want your daily life to reflect (For example: Presence, health, impact, family, creativity).
[P]lanning	Jeff stopped separating "work" from "life." He created an integrated plan that honored his responsibilities *and* his need for rest, joy, and growth. His calendar began to reflect his genuine priorities, not just his obligations.	Map your week as a whole human. Include work, caregiving, rest, relationships, and personal goals. Circle one area that needs more space and one that needs a limit. Adjust one thing in your schedule to reflect that shift.
[A]ction	Jeff made courageous choices about time and energy. He said no to draining commitments, set boundaries, and used tools (including AI) to handle tasks that didn't need his heart or creativity.	Identify one commitment, habit, or expectation you can say "no," "not now," or "not like this" to. Next, choose one tool or simple system (reminders, calendar, task app) to make your daily load lighter.

S.P.A.R.K. Pillar	How Jeff Used It	How You Can Begin
[R]esults	Jeff started to track his whole-life results including his energy, mood, connection, clarity—not just paychecks or productivity. As his choices aligned with his values, both his peace and performance improved.	At the end of the week, ask: **"How did I feel? What gave me life? What drained me?"** Notice patterns. Purposefully do more of what helps you feel most like yourself.
[K]PI Knowledge	Jeff built in regular reflection, so he didn't drift back into autopilot. What he learned about himself began to shape how he led others—with more empathy, flexibility, and clarity.	Create a simple weekly or monthly check-in: 10–15 minutes to ask, **"What's working? What's not? What do I need now?"** Capture your answers in a journal or notes app so you can view your growth over time.

Reflection Prompt:

What belief are you ready to release in order to head into a new chapter?

____

____

How can you design your rise without abandoning your peace?

____

____

____

The **S.P.A.R.K. Framework™** doesn't apply to organizations, teams, or titles alone—it applies to you as a whole human. Every time we align our life with our values, our energy with our priorities, and our decisions with who we are becoming, we don't just change our schedule. We change our story. The people you lead—at home, at work, and in your community—have a chance to feel that shift alongside us.

While we will focus primarily on the **S.P.A.R.K. Framework™** from the context of leadership and organizational systems, there is an inner layer which I call the **S.P.A.R.K. Effect™ – For Individuals**, which allows individuals a chance to go on a personal journey into integration, identity, and inner wholeness. Always remember: The more whole you become, the more human your leadership becomes. And that's the kind of leader the world is looking for right now.

Quote to Close the Chapter:

"Your past may have helped shape you, but your next decision can define you—and transform every system you touch.

— Dr. Michelle Brown

Next Up: Chapter 3 – AI-Informed, Human-Centered Systems: Amplify Results. Protect People. Scale What Works.

Now that we have seen how internal systems either drain or deepen our leadership, it is time to explore ways to leverage tech that gives us back time. After all, you know that sustainable change isn't about trying harder—it's about building internal systems and structures that support the humans who live inside them.

In the next chapter, we're going to take this same lens to one of the most disruptive yet beneficial forces of our time: AI. We will determine what tools are more than a gimmick, and how to use it less as a replacement for human wisdom, and more as a tool that can return time, clarify signals, and scale what works. We will discover how to do this without sacrificing dignity, trust, or values.

It is time to design AI-informed, human-centered internal systems using the **S.P.A.R.K. Framework™ Ecosystem** so you can amplify results, protect your people, and build organizations that are future-ready while remaining deeply human at the same time.

CHAPTER 3 – AI-INFORMED, HUMAN-CENTERED SYSTEMS
AMPLIFY RESULTS. PROTECT PEOPLE. SCALE WHAT WORKS.

Every leader juggles competing priorities. They have a team that needs clarity, a growing list of initiatives, and a leadership team who is looking to them for results. Behind each of these areas are humans who have full lives that are impacted by every metric. The calendar is full. The inbox is loud and the internal systems that were supposed to help keep us organized feel like one more thing to manage. Have you been there?

In today's modern world, when discussing the overwhelm, it is inevitable that someone will make the comment, "We should be using AI for this."

Take a moment to let that statement wash over you. How does it make you feel? The answer is vital as we move forward.

You see, for some leaders, that sentence lands like a threat. For others, it surfaces like a lifeline. For many, it only adds another question to an already crowded mind. *But how does that help me now?* They might wonder. For them, it is easiest to push such a comment to the back of their mind and ignore it.

The truth is AI has arrived at the same time that many of our internal systems already feel strained.

Performance reviews, communication channels, handoff processes, knowledge management, organizational culture-building—most of these were built for a slower, simpler, and more predictable world. Now, the allure of AI brings a new mix into the conversation. If not done well, bringing AI into the scene can mean layering powerful tools on top of disorganized structures that weren't designed for this level of complexity.

Therefore, I have found that the introduction of AI can either accelerate the harm or accelerate the healing.

It is up to us to ensure that we steer our teams toward tools which help versus harm. To do so, it is important that we dive into the topic of AI.

Within this chapter we are going to focus on **CoEvolution™**—how humans, internal systems, and AI can grow together. Our goal is to proceed in a way that amplifies what's good, repairs what's broken, and refuses to trade people's dignity for efficiency.

Wherever your thoughts and feelings are about AI, you are welcome in this conversation:

1. If you carry a **scarcity mindset**, wondering, "Will AI replace my role or my team?"

    This chapter provides a path to protect your people while still moving forward.

2. If you're **curious but unsure**, thinking, "I know there's potential in these tools, I just don't know where to start without making a mess."

    Consider this your grounded, human-centered on-ramp.

3. If you're the **tester**, already experimenting with tools in pockets of the organization, but haven't found the right blend of tech yet.

    This will help you discover structure, guardrails, and clarity so pilot programs don't feed chaos.

4. If you sit in the **fully adopted** camp and your organization has rolled out AI policies and procedures, yet you're wondering, "Is AI aligned with our values? Are we doing this the right way?"

I would like to invite you to use the **S.P.A.R.K. Framework™** to assess, refine, and realign for solutions, driven by actionable results.

No matter your perspective on this discussion, here's the bottom line: AI is not "the answer." Internal systems are not "the answer." Humans leading with grounded clarity and values—using both wisely—is where the authentic transformation lives and the answer lies to moving toward your goal.

That's why this conversation is not centered on AI *versus* humans, or AI *instead of* your existing internal systems. Our goal is to merge the two into **AI-informed, human-centered systems**. Inside of this approach, technology supports your people, not the other way around. As such, AI irrigates the field, but humans decide what to plant, how to tend it, and when to harvest.

Here Is How:

Most leaders don't struggle with ideas; they struggle with **capacity**:

1. Data piles up faster than anyone can read it.
2. Decisions lag because the right people are overloaded.
3. The team is doing the "right" things—just in a hard, slow, and manual way.

AI shortens the distance between **signal and decision**.

It can:

- Turn messy inputs into clear, easy-to-read summaries.
- Surface hidden trends across teams, clients, or consumers.
- Draft the first version, allowing you to refine instead of starting from scratch.

- Keep institutional knowledge intact, no matter who comes and goes from the team.
- Streamline internal processes, checkpoints, and enhance your current internal systems for updated successes.

But there's a line we do **not** cross:

- AI is not a substitute for **judgment, consent, or accountability**.
- Tech models can detect a pattern, but only a leader can decide what's ethical, wise, or aligned with the organization's values.
- An internal system can draft a message, but only a human can speak with wisdom when stakes are high and real-life decisions need to be made in real time.

When an organization forgets any of these facts, trust erodes from the inside and ripples outward. Customers feel mishandled, not helped. Employees feel replaced, not respected. Organizational cultures turn brittle—and results suffer.

Harmful Or Helpful? How To Gauge:

<u>**AI helps when it is a...**</u>	<u>**AI hurts when it is a...**</u>
Pattern finder—helping you discover themes regarding feedback, performance, and emotion faster.	Stand-in for leadership, mentorship, or consent.
Draft accelerator—giving you something intelligent to begin with, instead of a blank page.	Excuse to remove people from critical decision-making.
Decision *support*—surfacing options and risks you might otherwise miss, while it refrains from making the final call.	Black box you "just trust" because it sounds smart.
Translation layer—turning complex data into easily accessible insight.	Replacement for human judgment, care, or accountability.

My advice?

If you can't explain how a tool helps versus hurts, don't rely on it.

If you can't override the tool with human insight, don't deploy it.

Naming how AI helps or hurts sets the tone, but more is needed in order to utilize these tools the right way. You also need guardrails that protect your people when the pressure is high and the timelines are tight, yet the tool is not user friendly or intuitive. This is why we must plant a flag. The **S.P.A.R.K. Stance™** regarding how to leverage AI is key. These aren't suggestions, they are non-negotiable boundaries that keep your internal systems human-centered, even as your tools evolve. No matter how advanced AI becomes, these are the lines that don't move.

AI: Guardrails That Keep Your Organization Safe:

<u>AI Guardrail</u>	<u>What The Guardrail Does</u>	<u>Why It Matters</u>
Augment, don't erase.	Critical human-centric roles—such as mentors, clinicians, educators, community voices, and leaders—are supported by AI, not replaced by it. AI handles tasks. Humans hold the relationship, judgment, and accountability.	This guardrail protects jobs with purpose, preserves wisdom, and informs your people that they are valued, versus expendable.
Dignity by design.	People know when and how AI is being used. You're clear about data sources, purpose, and limits. No sneaky surveillance and no hidden use lurks in your hallways.	This guardrail builds trust. When humans feel informed and respected, tech adoption increases and resistance decreases.
Explainability over mystery.	Leaders can describe, in plain language, how an AI-driven recommendation was made, what benefit it provided, and what logic or organizational process it was based on.	This guardrail keeps you out of "the model said so" rationale and anchors decisions in accurate due process, versus blind dependence.
Bias checks as a habit.	You regularly test for bias, document findings, adjust, and retest. This occurs especially when equity, access, and opportunity are impacted.	This guardrail prevents past bias from being automated into your future systems and decisions.
Safety & privacy first.	You use safeguard data, define who can see what and for how long, and follow clear policies for access and retention.	This guardrail reduces risk, honors privacy, and shows your team and customers that information is not a shortcut. Instead, it is to be stewarded with care.
Human "veto" power.	A human can pause, question, escalate, or override AI decisions, always. The final say stays with a person, not a model.	This guardrail ensures AI never becomes the "boss." It centers ethical, relational, and contextual judgment where it belongs—with humans.

These guardrails take time to define within your organization, but they are not intended to slow innovation. Instead, they ensure alignment on the way you innovate. They inform your organization, as one, about who you are, what you value, and how you want your people to be treated. In turn, this allows your people to treat your customers with the same level of clarity and care. Altogether, once defined, this should rapidly elevate your innovation versus halt it.

Guardrails define what you will not compromise, no matter how impressive technology becomes. After reviewing the list, some may wonder, "Should we use AI in our organization at all—and if we do, are we doing it for the right reasons?"

To help with that, consider using the **AI Decision Filter™**. Think of it as your quick, repeatable gut-check before you say yes to leveraging AI in any project. It equips you to slow down long enough to ask better questions. This pause limits you from implementing technology that looks smart, but could erode trust, equity, or focus.

With this, we have a chance to ensure we are considering our:
- Purpose
- People
- Consumers
- Proven Track Records
- Processes
- Protective Stance

The AI Decision Filter™

(Use this before greenlighting any AI project.)

Filter	Guiding Question	Pausing To Answer Ensures That:
Purpose	Which **S.P.A.R.K.** outcome does this tool advance?	You're not using AI because it's trendy. The project should clearly support a **[S]**trategy, **[P]**lanning, **[A]**ction, **[R]**esults, or **[K]**PI Knowledge goal.
People	Who benefits from using this tool? Could anyone be harmed or excluded if we implement it in our organization?	Humans are at the center. It forces you to consider impact on employees, customers, and communities—not just efficiency or savings.
Proof	Beyond speed or cost, what evidence will show the tool is working?	You are not simply chasing "faster" and "cheaper." It clarifies what meaningful success looks like (e.g., equity, satisfaction, accuracy, retention).
Process	Where does human decision-making occur in the process—and where can override happen when needed?	There is always a person who is accountable for the final decision. It means that AI supports—not replaces—judgment, context, and intuition.
Protection	How will we check for bias, protect privacy, and prevent misuse of this tool over time?	Safety is built into the foundation from the start. It creates due process for how to monitor harm, protect data, and correct issues instead of hoping they don't happen.

Pausing to answer each of these filter questions keeps AI grounded in organizational values, not hype.

Once you've worked through the **AI Decision Filter™** to decide **if** a project is worth pursuing, the next question is: "Are we using AI in a way that truly helps or are we quietly causing harm?"

This is not always easy. We must take a hard look in the mirror to find out how our processes are limiting us or accelerating our goals. It takes courage to determine the line.

The difference often comes down to one simple distinction:

1. Are you using AI to **augment** your people?
2. Or are you using it to **replace** them?

On paper, both paths can look efficient. However, in practice, they create completely different organizational cultures, customer experiences, and long-term outcomes.

How AI Augments vs. Replaces:

Area	When AI Supports (Augmentation)	When AI Damages (Replacement)
Time & Focus	AI should create speed with sense. A team member could spend one hour of sifting through data, or they could leverage a tool in five minutes and gain clarity easily—leveraging their time for human review. In this scenario, people get more time for creativity.	AI can dehumanize experiences by favoring speed. When bots "handle" grief, conflict, or complex needs, both customers and employees feel dismissed.
Consistency & Quality	AI should provide consistent quality without rigidity. Standardized quality levels are captured, ensuring that excellence isn't dependent on heroics or memory, but is documented accurately.	AI can increase hidden bias at scale: Yesterday's inequities become tomorrow's automated decisions—now happening faster, to more people, with less visibility.
Access to Information	AI should increase access and not be a tool for gatekeeping. People find answers fast. Action isn't delayed because a single source of information is busy.	AI can hold quality & safety risks. When approval, diagnosis, or hiring is automated without human veto, harm is likely, and liability increases.
Culture & Care	AI should provide focus, not surveillance. The goal is for AI to remove administrative noise, allowing humans to spend time on coaching relationships, mentoring, and creative work.	AI does cultural damage when it attempts to replace mentorship or human connection. This signals that wisdom is optional. People disengage, shut down, or leave.

So, what am I saying? In short, anytime AI is used, it becomes a multiplier—for helping or hurting. Whatever you leverage it for—care or convenience, quick fix or consumer support, equity or shortcuts, wisdom or speed-at-all-costs—it amplifies.

That's why the discussion must move beyond only answering the question of, "Are we using AI?" and go deeper. The real question is: **"What are we asking AI to multiply?**

How do we move this discussion into real-world scenarios that you and I face daily?

Let's find what is possible by leveraging the **S.P.A.R.K.** pillars to see how we can use AI as a force multiplier to grow our organization.

AI Use plus Human Role Integration:

S.P.A.R.K. Pillar	How AI Supports This Pillar	Human Role / Leadership Focus
[S]trategy – Better vision, fewer opinions.	AI is used to sift feedback, market chatter, engagement data, and internal notes, allowing team members to see themes sooner and spot patterns that matter. It shortens the distance between noise and signal.	Once sifted, a human chooses the direction. Leaders decide what the patterns *mean*, which priorities to set, and how strategy aligns with values, purpose, and people.
[P]lanning – Plans that respect reality.	AI reveals capacity limits, risky dependencies, and likely blockers across teams and timelines. This allows team members to plan with actual constraints, not wishful thinking.	Once elements are revealed by AI, a human decides the trade-offs. Leaders determine what to delay, what to resource, and how to protect people from burnout while still moving the mission forward.
[A]ction – Return time to where it matters.	AI handles the flow of work. It does the routing, summarizing, drafting, reminding, and organizing of information allowing team members to focus time on high-value tasks.	With tasks organized, humans are kept at the center. Leaders protect time for judgment, creativity, coaching, relationship-building, and care, versus simply being engaged in task completion.
[R]esults – Proof people can see.	AI assembles simple, human-readable "chart and story" views from complex data. It allows progress, risks, and wins to be visible in real time.	With increased visibility, you get to interpret the data and act accordingly. Leaders give meaning to the numbers, communicate the story, celebrate the right wins, and make course corrections. Models don't take the victory lap—you do.
[K]PI Knowledge – Learning that lives.	AI auto-tags lessons, decisions, examples, and best practices into a searchable knowledge base. This pooling of learnings alleviates the burden of curation from team members' mental load or from filling their inboxes.	Once curated, you get to teach. Leaders decide what becomes part of the playbook, what needs to be taught, and how to turn information into shared wisdom and culture.

AI has the ability to strengthen every **S.P.A.R.K.** Pillar. Yet this is only true when humans stay in the lead, leveraging technology to support strategy versus replace the professionals who allow the organization to thrive.

You may wonder: *So where do I begin?*

I want you to start small, on purpose. The goal isn't to overwhelm your organization with tools. Instead, it's to choose one meaningful place for AI to return time, increase clarity, and strengthen your people.

My advice?

Choose one area to pilot first by circling the areas most aligned with.

AI-Informed, Human-Centered Systems Cheat Sheet

<u>If you want to…</u>

Make sense of feedback, surveys, or stakeholder input faster…	…use AI to summarize comments, group themes, and highlight patterns you can review with your team.
Plan more realistically across teams…	…use AI to map workloads, timelines, and dependencies so you can see bottlenecks before they happen.
Reduce admin overload…	…use AI to draft emails, create meeting notes, summarize documents, and route tasks—combined with human review.
Show impact clearly to stakeholders…	…use AI to pull data from multiple systems into simple dashboards and narrative summaries.
Capture learning so it doesn't walk out the door…	…use AI to tag decisions, best practices, and lessons learned into searchable knowledge hubs.

Once you've circled one area from the cheat sheet, your goal is to test it in a way that feels safe, human, and aligned with your values. You don't need a massive rollout or a full tech stack to begin. You need a thoughtful, low-risk starting point that lets your team experience the benefits of AI without feeling like an experiment themselves. As you begin to discover what this means for you as a leader, here's a quick five-minute bias check you can ask yourself to get clearer guidance before taking your best next step.

Five-Minute Bias Check (Fast & Real)

Before you scale anything, ask yourself:

- Who is not represented by the data we used?
- Do results differ by group (race, gender, age, location, role)?
- Could a non-expert understand how this recommendation was made?
- Can a human override this quickly and easily?
- Have we ethically informed our people how their data was used—and why?

While these simple check-ins do not replace deeper audits, they do ensure that equity and ethics remain on the table from the very beginning. Let's take a look at a quick assessment below.

AI S.P.A.R.K. Systems Readiness Assessment

To help you move from ideas to action, our team has created an **AI S.P.A.R.K. Systems Readiness Assessment**. This provides you with a quick online diagnostic which enables you to:

- Identify which internal systems are outdated or disconnected.
- See where AI can support **[S]**trategy, **[P]**lanning, **[A]**ction, **[R]**esults, and **[K]**PI Knowledge.

- Receive a simple PDF report with insights on your personalized **S.P.A.R.K.** aligned next steps.

You can access this assessment online and receive your personalized report by scanning the QR code.

Our hope is that you are able to use this chapter and the assessment together as a playbook to accelerate your goals. We are rooting for you to build an **AI-informed, human-centered system** that amplifies results, protects people, and scales your entire organization in the direction you want it to go.

Quote to Close the Chapter:

Let AI carry the load but allow people to carry the meaning. That's the S.P.A.R.K. way—internal systems work hard, while humans lead with heart.

— Dr. Michelle Brown

SCAN TO TAKE The S.P.A.R.K. Framework **Assessment™**

Next Up: Chapter 4 – [S]trategy: Lead with Vision, Not Reaction

You've just seen how AI and internal systems can either drain or deepen your leadership. You've also seen that the real power isn't in the tools themselves; it's in the humans who decide why they're used, where they're placed, and what they're allowed to shape.

That's why the next step in your **S.P.A.R.K. Framework™** journey is [S]trategy—not as a buzzword, but as a compass.

You're not just here to "use AI better."

You're here to **lead better**—with vision, not reaction.

In Chapter 4, it's time to focus on your **Strategy**. This isn't just about personal direction; it's about strategic transformation that bridges your individual clarity with internal systematic change. We'll explore what it really means to **lead with vision, not reaction.** You'll learn how to define a purpose-driven direction that anchors your goals and decisions—personally and professionally. You'll discover how to identify outdated strategic approaches, design transitional strategies that work in the real world, and create systematic change that feels empowering rather than overwhelming.

Let's begin with the [S]trategy that aligns your leadership with your legacy and start leading the future on purpose.

CHAPTER 4 – [S]TRATEGY
LEAD WITH VISION, NOT REACTION

Change doesn't just happen, it's directed. It's a process that must be guided and shaped. To help us maneuver that process, we begin with **[S]** pillar for **Strategy**, in our **S.P.A.R.K. Framework™ Ecosystem**. Strategy that directs change is more than a list of goals. It's a bold decision to lead with purpose. To land success, this elevated form of strategy must remain anchored in values and be aligned to a clear vision of what's next.

Have you ever sat in a strategy session and felt like it completely missed the mark?

That is because typical strategy attempts are built on outdated assumptions regarding how change happens, how organizations function, and what values lead people to make decisions. It is time to move beyond typical quarterly reviews, traditional annual goal-setting approaches, reactive pivots based on market conditions, or, let's face it, meetings that are filled with sophisticated guessing that lead to nowhere. These methods were designed for a predictable world that no longer exists.

Instead, it is time to adopt strategy that does not seek to predict the future, instead, it carries an adaptive capacity that can respond to the future while staying grounded in authentic purpose.

When I was challenged by my high school teachers to take a hard look at who I was becoming, I can now see that I was smack in the middle of the opportunity to make a very clear mental decision to change with intent. That started a path where I defined a distinct vision for the type of lifestyle I desired for myself. What I didn't realize then was that I was letting go of an outdated mindset—the internal system—which was a reactive, disruptive pattern that had been driving my behavior and replaced it with a strategic, purpose-driven approach to my own development. The change went deeper than shifting my actions. I redesigned the internal framework that allowed me to embody those actions.

In short, I rebuilt a new strategy for my life that embodied a holistic approach, not separate aspects.

I used the same approach when I decided to become class president and later graduate with honors from high school and college. That choice was fueled by strategy, even when I did not recognize it at the time. Looking back, my choice looked less like setting goals and creating action plans. Instead, it was a reorientation toward vision-driven decision-making, rather than reaction-based responses to my circumstances. Each of us can take strategy to this same level of depth that changes who we are at the core.

From this lens, strategy becomes a stabilizing choice you lean on each time you need to pivot or re-align. After all, in our current business environments and in life, uncertainty isn't the exception—it's the new normal. Leaders who thrive aren't the ones with the most detailed five-year plans. They are the ones who have the strongest strategic thinking muscles and the most adaptive frameworks for decision-making, in life and business.

Consider Elena, the director of operations at a mid-sized tech company. Elena felt she was constantly firefighting instead of truly leading. Her experience is a common one, which highlights how outdated internal systems and reactive organizational cultures keep even the most capable leaders stuck in survival mode.

As we get to know her, we are going to view Elena's story through the lens of [S]trategy.

Because what ultimately transformed her leadership—and her organization—wasn't just working harder or adopting new tools. Elena took back her life as she made the strategic decision to stop reacting to everyone else's moves and start defining a clear, human-centered and focused direction of her own.

Elena's approach to strategy was reactive. When she saw what competitors were doing, her team would analyze quarterly results and scramble to adjust their approaches. Over time, Elena realized that such a reactive pattern had created exactly the chaos they wanted to avoid.

Using the **S.P.A.R.K. Framework™**, Elena didn't just change her personal approach to strategic thinking—she transformed how her organization approached strategy development and change management. Instead of quarterly reaction cycles, they moved to continuous strategic sensing. Instead of copying competitor moves, they focused on amplifying their unique strengths. Instead of separating operational execution from strategic vision, they integrated both values into a seamless adaptive internal system.

The results spoke for themself. Within a single year, Elena's organization went from being stuck in constant crisis change management to shifting toward proactive opportunity creation. They stopped chasing market trends and started setting them. They moved from defensive positioning to innovative leadership in their industry. Elena proved that the shift from reactive to strategic thinking was not just a personal development goal—it can ripple outward to lead an organization-wide imperative.

<u>**Summary**</u>

Obstacle

As director of operations, Elena was stuck in constant firefighting. Strategy meant reacting to competitors and quarterly numbers, then scrambling. The team felt busy but not truly led.

Opportunity

The repeated crisis-response pattern became a turning point. Elena chose to see the chaos as data—a signal that their strategic "operating system" needed to change, not that people were failing.

Strategic S.P.A.R.K. Shift ([S]trategy)

Using the **S.P.A.R.K. Framework™**, Elena moved from quarterly reaction to continuous strategic sensing, shifted from copying competitors to amplifying their unique strengths, and wove strategy into daily operations so vision and execution finally matched.

Outcome

Within a year, the organization moved from playing defense to creating opportunities. They stopped chasing trends and started setting them. Elena proved that shifting from reactive to strategic thinking isn't just personal growth—it's an organizational gamechanger.

Elena dove deep into who she wanted to be—energized and present for her team—versus reactive. This in turn overflowed into who she was at home. Both sides of her benefited when she paused to determine what values would drive her decisions. Because here's the truth: We are one whole person—who we are at home impacts how we show up at work, and who we are at work impacts how we show up everywhere else.

It is crucial to stay grounded in your why. When things feel off, examine what strategic approaches you've inherited that may be sabotaging you or your team's successes. To re-center, go back to a root question: Does how I am operating align with the bigger picture of who I am or desire to be? Organizations can ask something similar. When something feels off, leadership teams must come together to determine: Are we operating from any outdated assumptions that no longer serve our current reality?

Answering these questions is where strategy steps in, not as just a buzz word, but as a compass which can authentically define the right next step. Sustainable change will always align individual authenticity with organizational purpose, personal values with professional excellence, and human-centered approaches with technological efficiency.

Let's dive into the story of one CEO who had to do just that.

Robert, a CEO of a family-owned manufacturing business, struggled to compete with larger corporations. He had been told the answer was to cut costs, automate processes, and compete on price, but Robert recognized that this strategy would eliminate exactly what made his company special: the humans working inside the organization. He cherished personal relationships, craft expertise, and community connection, which differentiated his company from others in the marketplace.

Instead of following outdated competitive strategies, Robert used the **S.P.A.R.K. Framework™** to develop an approach that amplified his organization's unique strengths.

[S]trategy led Robert to define his competitive advantage as *artisanal quality and community partnership* versus just cost efficiency. This meant he could stop the race to the bottom and provide a premium, values-aligned position in the market instead

Instead of following outdated competitive strategies, Robert used the **S.P.A.R.K. Framework™** to completely re-ground his **[S]**trategy. He started by asking a different set of questions:

- Who are we really here to serve?
- What do our best clients value most about us?
- What are we willing to *never* compromise, even if it costs us in the short term?

From those conversations with his team, long-term customers, and community partners, a new strategic truth emerged: Their real advantage wasn't speed or volume—it was trust, craftsmanship, and deep local roots.

So, Robert made a deliberate strategic choice:

- They would no longer try to win as the "cheapest or trendiest option."
- They would position themselves as the premium, high-trust, craft-focused partner for clients who cared about quality, reliability, and community impact.

That meant his **[S]**trategy became crystal clear:

- Compete on **artisanal quality and relationship**, not just price.
- Double down on **human skill + precision** instead of racing to replace people with machines.
- Tell a clear story in the market about **why they cost more** and what values that price protects: quality, jobs, community, and long-term reliability.

In other words, **[S]**trategy for Robert wasn't a slogan or a slide—it was a conscious decision about *who they are, who they serve, what they refuse to sacrifice, and how they will win differently* than everyone else trying to compete on cost versus human-centered focus areas. Such a strategy defied conventional business wisdom. Yet, with his company emerging as the premium choice in the market, they were able to increase prices and improve their margins. Though strategy was only the first step, Robert's success illustrates a crucial principle: The most powerful strategy isn't about outcompeting others using their rules or popular trends—it's about changing the game entirely by operating from your authentic strengths and consumer truths.

Do you know what is great about pausing to consider what your strategy will be and how it aligns with your core values? You get to define what success looks like for you. It is not defined by this quarter or market trends. Instead, it centers on the impact you desire and the legacy you are building. Sustainable strategy is never about short-term wins at the expense of long-term integrity. Instead, it is a creative approach that gets stronger over time, more effective under pressure, and more aligned with your evolving understanding of what matters most.

Let's put this into perspective with the scenarios below:

S.P.A.R.K. Framework™ – Strategy Thought Starter

Scenario: You feel stuck. You've been juggling a dozen responsibilities, personally and professionally, but no matter how much you achieve, you still feel you are chasing something undefined. Maybe your team isn't hitting its goals, or you're leading a business that's bringing in revenue but drifting from your original purpose. You have been adjusting, reacting, and trying to keep things afloat. Yet deep down, you're unsure where you are truly heading.

Sound familiar? You're not alone.

But what if outdated frameworks and old mindsets are keeping you locked in a cycle? What if applying linear thinking to complex challenges does not match what you need right now? What if Band-Aid level, short-term tactics are halting your long-term aspirations? I am here to let you know that the feeling of being stuck is not a personal failure. Instead, it's feedback that your current strategic approach has reached its limits. The mindset you have adopted along the way will no longer work for where you're trying to go.

But the good news is there is an opportunity to create change.

You have come to a moment that so many individuals, leaders, and entrepreneurs have felt, but may not have faced. Let me encourage you to sit with the frustration. See what the "stuck" is saying. Dare to pause and pivot with purpose. You have a chance to end the cycle of burnout combined with the hamster wheel effect and move beyond the burden of fear.

The difference between those who break through and those who break down isn't talent, resources, or luck—it's sourced in a willingness to examine and update their internal strategies and systems.

Let's face outdated beliefs and faulty strategy head-on. By peering into these mindsets, we can see the cost of remaining stuck along with what strategy shift is required of us.

<u>Outdated belief</u>	<u>How it shows up as an outdated strategy</u>	<u>What it costs you</u>	<u>The S.P.A.R.K. Shift</u>™
"If we just work harder, things will improve."	Pushing more hours, more hustle, more initiatives—without changing systems or strategy.	Burnout, turnover, and busy teams with little meaningful progress.	"If we change the internal systems, the work becomes streamlined intentionally." **How:** Focus on fixing structures, not squeezing people.

Outdated belief	How it shows up as an outdated strategy	What it costs you	The S.P.A.R.K. Shift™
"Good leaders have all the answers."	Strategy is built in closed rooms; decisions are made at the top with little input from the people closest to the work.	Blind spots, slow decisions, low buy-in, and missed innovation from your own team.	"Good leaders ask better questions." **How:** Co-create strategy with the people who live the reality every day.
"People should leave their personal life at the door."	Policies and practices ignore caregiving, mental health, identity, and real-life demands.	Disconnection, mistrust, and talent quietly opting out or leaving.	"We are whole humans everywhere we go." **How:** Design strategy and internal systems that respect the full human, not just the job title.
"If it worked before, it will work again."	Copying past playbooks, old tactics, or "industry best practices" without questioning if they still fit your context.	Stagnation, irrelevance, and constantly being surprised by change.	"What worked before is data, not a script." **How:** Use the past as input, but design strategy for *this* reality, not yesterday's.
"Our job is to keep up with competitors."	Watching what others do and reacting—matching prices, copying offers, chasing trends.	Always behind, constantly reactive, no clear identity or unique value.	"Our job is to lead from our strengths." **How:** Strategy starts with who *we* are and who we serve best, not with what others are doing.
"People are resources to be managed."	Headcount viewed only through cost and capacity; little focus on values, voice, or experience.	Low engagement, high turnover, and a culture where people survive but don't thrive.	"People are humans to be supported." **How:** Strategy centers human needs, motivation, and potential as core to performance.

Outdated belief	How it shows up as an outdated strategy	What it costs you	The S.P.A.R.K. Shift™
"Tech (or AI) will fix this for us."	Buying tools to patch broken processes; automating confusion; using AI to speed up flawed systems.	Faster chaos, trust issues, and wasted money on tools no one uses well.	"Tech should support healthy systems." **How:** Fix the strategy and process first, then add tools to amplify what works.
"We don't have time to step back and rethink things."	Endless urgency, back-to-back crises, no space for reflection or strategic thinking.	Chronic firefighting, exhaustion, and repeating the same problems in new packaging.	"We can't afford *not* to step back." **How:** Pausing to think strategically is part of the work, not a luxury.

When you update a belief, this will naturally update strategy. That's where genuine transformation begins. Strategy is not found in a new tool or trend. Instead, it is founded in a new way of seeing yourself, your people, and what's possible.

S.P.A.R.K. Framework™ Solution-Based Approach:

Strategy starts at the core. To begin, I would like to invite you to "dare to pause". Set aside 20 minutes to reflect on what form of strategy you have adopted—and if you would like to update it.

To begin, ask yourself:

What am I doing this for—really?

____

____

What beliefs about success, achievement, or professional growth are driving my current approach?

____

____

Are any of them outdated or misaligned to my current culture? If so, which ones?

____

____

Does my approach still serve the vision I have for my life, my team, or my mission? If so, how?

____

____

Is any part of my leadership operating from inherited strategies that served someone else's vision in a different era? If so, which ones?

____

____

If I keep going at this pace, what outcome do I expect?

____

____

What systemic changes do I need to pursue to ensure that my daily actions are aligned with my long-term vision?

____

____

As you review your answers, recognize you have a chance to align your daily actions with your deeper "why." In doing so, you get to stop reacting to what's urgent and start designing what's important. More than that—you abandon past approaches as permanent realities. You get to operate from systematic alternatives that serve your authentic goals. The result? You turn chaos into clarity, burnout into boundaries, and business into meaningful movement.

That's the power of strategy. It's anchored in _you_.

Consider the transformation Maya experienced. As a nonprofit director, she felt trapped between donor expectations and community needs. Traditional nonprofit strategy suggested adapting programs to match funding opportunities, even when those programs didn't address the most pressing community issues. Maya recognized that this approach was not just strategically limiting—it was ethically problematic.

Starting with the **[S]** in the **S.P.A.R.K. Framework™**, Maya developed a strategy that prioritized community impact while building sustainable funding models. By pausing to reflect on her values and what beliefs she wanted to guide her, Maya was able to redefine success metrics to include community voice and long-term systemic change.

She abandoned an old belief that told her the only thing that mattered was total dollars raised and number of services delivered.

Maya stepped back and re-grounded her **[S]**trategy. Instead of asking, "What do donors want to fund?" she began with a bolder question: "What does our community actually need and what are we here to change long term?" From there, she made a conscious strategic decision: community impact would lead, funding would follow. She redefined success so it wasn't just about "total dollars raised" or "number of services delivered," but about the depth of transformation:

- Are the right people being reached?
- Are root causes being addressed, not just symptoms?
- Are community members informing and shaping what we do and not just receiving services?

Strategically, this meant:

- Naming **community voice and long-term systemic change** as core success metrics.
- Choosing to **pursue partners and donors who aligned** with those priorities, even if it meant saying no to misaligned money.
- Positioning the organization as a **mission-first, community-led partner**, not just a service provider chasing grants.

In other words, Maya's **[S]**trategy shifted from "follow the funding" to "lead with impact and invite the right funding to join us." As Maya moved through the **S.P.A.R.K. Framework™ Ecosystem**, the results transformed not just Maya's organization but influenced their entire funding ecosystem. Donors began appreciating the authentic impact of data and community testimonials. Other nonprofits started adopting similar approaches. Maya proved that strategic authenticity was not just ethically superior—it also proved to be most effective at creating sustainable organizational success.

To make Maya's transformation tangible and to find similarities in how her story applies to your own, let's dive into her Obstacle → Opportunity → Option → Outcome.

Summary

Obstacle	As a nonprofit director, Maya felt trapped between donor expectations and real community needs. Strategy had quietly become "follow the funding," even when programs didn't truly address the most urgent issues on the ground.
Opportunity	The tension between what donors wanted and what the community needed became a turning point. Instead of blaming lack of funding, Maya treated the misalignment as data that their strategic lens—and definition of success—needed to change.

<u>**Summary**</u>

Strategic S.P.A.R.K. Shift ([S]trategy)	Maya shifted her **[S]**trategy from, "What will donors pay for?" to "What is our community here to change and who will partner with that?" She redefined success around community voice and long-term impact and chose to seek funders aligned with that mission.
Outcome	Over time, programs became more targeted and impactful, donors valued the authenticity of the results, and other nonprofits began modeling her approach. Maya proved that mission-first, community-led strategy isn't just ethical—it's more effective, sustainable and durable.

Maya's story reveals that when **[S]**trategy is anchored in truth and community, you don't just change programs—you change ecosystems and lives.

Earlier, I invited you to pause to define what beliefs you may have adopted that were creating obstacles in your life. Now it's your turn to determine what your core approach is for **[S]**trategy. As you answer, feel free to apply each question to a scenario that best defines where you are currently.

[S]trategy: The Core Approach

1. Define Your Why

What drives your motivation?

- What are you working for?
- What satisfaction does it give you personally?
- Who else does your labor serve (your family, your team, your clients, your community)?
- Why do your actions matter *now*, in this season of your life or leadership?
- Which inherited assumptions about success (titles, money, perfection, pace, "looking the part") are driving your actions?

Your reflections:

____

____

____

____

2. Visualize the Future

Imagine a new mindset and updated strategy is already in place.

- Imagine this change or goal as it is already a reality—what do you see?
- What's different about your day-to-day life or leadership?
- Who is impacted—and how?
- What outdated internal systems, habits, or expectations have been replaced with these fresh, sustainable alternatives?

Your reflections:

____

____

____

____

3. Identify Obstacles

Name what's in the way—honestly.

1. What internal obstacles (fears, beliefs, patterns, etc.) are in the way right now?
2. What external obstacles (systems, structures, expectations, etc.) are in the way right now?
3. What beliefs, internal systems, or structures must shift for these obstacles to be eradicated and a new future possible?
4. Which of these barriers are based in outdated approaches disguised as "realistic limitations"?

Your reflections:

____

____

____

____

4. Set Direction, Not Goals

Direction gives your decisions a compass.

1. Instead of asking, "What's my next goal?", ask, "What direction am I committed to move toward?"

2. In one sentence, how would you describe the direction you're heading?

3. How can your direction integrate technological efficiency with human-centered values? (For example: what tools and internal systems can you leverage to support people versus replace them?)

4. What one decision will you make this week to align with this direction?

Your reflections:

____

____

____

____

Here's what we have come to realize: Without a strategy, we are just reacting. But with strategy, we are intentionally designing. We don't rise to new levels through reaction; we rise by intentional design. And as we strategically identify what needs to change, we create clear pathways for ourselves that allow crucial and necessary change to happen.

[S]trategy is the first pillar of our proven **S.P.A.R.K. Framework™** because it shapes every other step we take. It informs what we plan, how we act, what we measure, how we grow, and most importantly, how we pivot during times of change and uncertainty. It offers structure and boundaries, which guide us to pivot and evolve with confidence, versus emotional reactivity.

[S]trategy in Practice

For Organizations and Teams

Professional Strategy Exercise – Leading with Vision

What's a current challenge your team or organization is facing?

____

____

And what outdated organizational systems or processes might be contributing to this challenge?

What's your strategic vision for resolving this challenge?

How does this vision integrate technological efficiency with human-centered approaches?

Who are the key stakeholders you need to align with and why?

Which stakeholders might resist change because they're invested in current internal systems, and how will you address this?

What resources or mindset shifts are needed to move forward?

What internal systems or processes need to be updated or replaced to support your strategic vision?

What's the best next decision you can make that aligns with this vision?

____

____

And how will you ensure this decision creates sustainable change rather than temporary improvement?

____

____

For Leaders

Legacy-Focused Strategy Alignment

What is the lasting impact you want your leadership to have on your team or organization?

____

____

What outdated leadership approaches do you need to release to create this impact?

____

____

What values are non-negotiable in the way you lead?

____

____

How do these values challenge conventional leadership practices in your industry or organization?

____

____

How do your daily decisions reflect or contradict the vision you hold?

Where are you still operating from inherited leadership patterns rather than conscious strategic choices?

Where do you need more alignment between intention and execution?

What internal systems or processes do you need to implement to ensure this alignment is sustainable?

What is one courageous decision you can make today to lead with greater strategic purpose?

And how will this decision model the kind of strategic thinking you want to see throughout your organization?

For Coaches and Consultants

Client-Centered Strategy Mapping

Who is your ideal client and what transformation are they seeking?

____

____

And what outdated approaches in your industry are preventing clients from achieving this transformation?

____

____

What is your "why" for doing this work beyond revenue?

____

____

How does your unique background and experience differentiate your approach from generic industry standards?

____

____

What limiting beliefs or patterns have stopped your clients—or you—from scaling?

____

____

Which of these limitations are actually outdated business models disguised as "market realities"?

____

____

What future success do you want to see for your clients and for your business?

____

____

How does this vision integrate technology for efficiency while maintaining the human connection that creates real transformation?

What strategic offer, content, or client experience will you create to bridge that gap?

And how will this strategic approach replace scattered service delivery with focused expertise?

For Individuals

Personal Strategy Exercise – Vision Mapping

What change do you feel called to make in your personal life right now?

And what outdated beliefs about success, achievement, or personal growth might be holding you back?

Why does this change matter to you on a deeper level?

How does this personal change connect to broader transformations you want to see in your professional or community life?

What does success look like for you six months from now?

And how does this definition of success reflect your authentic values rather than external expectations?

What internal beliefs or habits might be holding you back?

Which of these patterns are inherited from outdated cultural, family, or professional conditioning?

What's the ONE strategic action step you can take this week to begin?

And how will this action create momentum for systematic change rather than just temporary improvement?

Chapter Wrap-Up

When you lead with strategy, you reclaim your power to shape the future. You stop reacting to what life hands you, and you start designing what you deserve. More importantly, you stop accepting outdated internal systems as permanent realities and start creating sustainable alternatives that serve your authentic goals and values.

You have now identified your "why," envisioned your ideal outcomes, and started to shift your mindset toward acting with intention. You've also examined which inherited approaches need updating and designed transitional strategies that honor both stability and growth. That's not just strategy; it is a commitment to rise with clarity and conviction, not chaos.

But here is what I know: A vision without a plan is just a dream and a strategy without structure is just talk. When strategy systematically addresses outdated internal systems, while building sustainable alternatives, vision becomes an inevitable reality.

To bring your vision to life, you need a clear **[P]**lan, and you will revisit that **[P]**lan over and over and over again. Why? Because life will demand that you adapt to seen and unforeseen changing circumstances. But there is good news—because we paused to define our "why" and mark out our own **[S]**trategy, we can stay anchored in our purpose.

That is how I graduated from my university with honors among other successes, personally and professionally. Even amid numerous life challenges, which demanded I pivot, I was able to stay the course. Since my teachers challenged me to determine who I wanted to be—I held to that path. I was able to graduate as an honor roll student and as a student-athlete who worked throughout the year (including my sports season). I became the first in my family to get a scholarship to play at the D-1 level and was named an All-American, the second in the history of that university for my sport. I graduated from my master's program a year early and completed my doctorate program with honors as a new wife and mother of two, while also landing my first 6-figure paying career in corporate.

I held to my core beliefs—and you can too.

This is how thousands of leaders, organizations, and consultants have transformed their approaches from reactive management to strategic leadership, from scattered activity to focused impact, from inherited limitations to conscious design.

To continue your journey, let's dive into how you can go deeper into the **S.P.A.R.K. Framework™** and put **[P]**lanning on your side.

Quote to Close the Chapter:

"A vision without a plan is just a dream, and a strategy without structure is just talk

— Dr. Michelle Brown

Next Up: Chapter 5 – [P]lanning: Map Backwards, Move Forward

Planning is where the power of your purpose becomes practical. We get to transform your strategy into structured, actionable steps that keep you focused, motivated, and aligned. Together, we will go beyond traditional planning and into "the how" of replacing outdated approaches with sustainable alternatives.

You deserve planning approaches that honor both individual authenticity and organizational effectiveness, ones that integrate technological efficiency with human-centered values, and ones that create real internal system changes without sacrificing what matters most, humans.

Ready to take the power of your vision and give it structure? Let's transform timelines and goals into actions you can see and feel. Move your purpose into a **[P]**lan to build a future you're proud to walk into. It is time for your values, your people, and your authentic vision to transform what's possible.

CHAPTER 5 – [P]LANNING
MAP BACKWARDS, MOVE FORWARD!

In the last chapter, we talked about building on strategy by creating structure. This takes us directly into **[P]**lanning, i.e. putting timelines and milestones in place to harness your momentum and become unstoppable. But let's be honest: This is where many of us feel stuck. It is easy to get caught up in motion but lack actual movement. We know where we want to go, but the "how" seems overwhelming. I know that for me, when details get blurry, that is when a voice of doubt creeps in. But let me remind you: There is no such thing as perfect.

Traditional planning approaches built on outdated assumptions miss the core of how change happens in complex organizations or dynamic markets. Linear planning models—including five-year strategic plans, annual budget cycles, and quarterly goal cascades—only work in predictable environments that simply don't exist anymore.

Typical "planning" is often just sophisticated scheduling with endless meetings that lead to nowhere. When it is layered with outdated project management frameworks that ignore the human dynamics or the technological possibilities of our current reality, we lack what we need to be successful. After all, planning isn't about creating detailed roadmaps for uncertain futures—it's about building adaptive internal systems that navigate any terrain while maintaining strategic direction, with intention.

It is time to retire the saying that "practice makes perfect." It doesn't. Practice makes progress. Besides **[P]**lanning isn't about perfection. It's about moving forward with clarity, flexibility, and intention with room to pivot. It's how we create adaptive planning systems that get stronger with each iteration.

Perhaps you have heard the phrase, "If you fail to plan, you plan to fail." To me, this is more than a catchy quote. It's something many of us have faced. I also believe that if you plan using outdated frameworks, mindsets, strategies and processes, you plan for stagnant irrelevance.

Here's a quick S.P.A.R.K. Snapshot™ to refer to as you create your plan:

	<u>**Outdated Frameworks**</u>	<u>**Outdated Strategies**</u>	<u>**Outdated Processes**</u>
What it is	"Hidden rules" and beliefs that lurk in the background define how you *think* about work, success, and people.	Past big-picture approaches break when your team, season, or market changes.	Systems, routines, and workflows that shape how work gets done day-to-day, yet create continual distress.
What it looks like	Common sayings such as: "If we just work harder, it will get better." "Leave your personal life at the door." "This is how it's always been done here." "Leave it to the leaders, they have all the answers." "Around here, people are resources first, and humans second."	Decision-makers chase competitors instead of defining their own lane. Leaders build plans to get short-term numbers, not long-term direction. We copy "best practices" without asking if they fit our reality or values. You set goals with no clear *why* behind them. Team members react to every crisis instead of acting from a clear vision.	Performance review meetings feel like a box to check, versus a real conversation. Long meetings that end without reaching clarity or making decisions toward action. Needing 17 approvals to move one idea forward. Burning out on manual tasks that could be automated. Top-down communication that leaves teams in the dark.

[P]lanning is meant to energize, not stagnate creativity or action. It is not meant to be a rigid structure that boxes you in. Instead, it must be engineered to provide a flexible foundation that lets you pivot, adapt, and grow with you. The **S.P.A.R.K. Framework™** recognizes these needs. It seeks to use and integrate technological efficiency with human-centered approaches, therefore building a systematic structure that carries adaptive flexibility and individual authenticity to enhance organizational effectiveness.

With this framework, you don't have to restart or react, you simply adjust.

[P]lanning is about small directional steps. For me, that always meant starting at the end and working backward. To be clear, this does not mean working backward from goals. Instead, I see it as working backward from the impact I want to create. I start by imagining the internal systems I want to see in place, the culture I want to build, and the legacy I want to leave behind.

What was my desired end goal?

What life did I want to live?

What kind of impact did I want to leave behind?

To answer this, I must also determine what outdated approaches I have regarding my understanding of what achievement and success is and is not. Once I can see that clearly, I can determine what I need to release in order to create sustainable, authentic progress and pivot with ease.

At the time I didn't know what the answer was, but what I did know was where I wanted to go and that was enough for me.

I was fortunate to have key people in my life that believed in who I was and who I "could be"—often more than I could even see at the time. But they never stopped guiding me, even when things appeared "bad". Their questions challenged me to take inspired action and sparked who I had become and how I truly wanted to be represented. This is where **[P]**lanning ignited my best next step and elevated that reality, not only for myself but those I serve as an Industrial and Organizational Psychologist expert as well.

As a young woman, I was determined to take steps forward—steps that empowered me and proved any doubters wrong. The doubters included my own internal system, my outdated mindset, detractors, or anyone that did not think outside of the box. I knew that I wanted to be someone I was proud of and continue to be the leader that others already viewed me as. As I continued **[P]**lanning, I realized various contributing factors that caused me to pause and reflect on if they were still aligned with where I planned to go or not.

In that moment, I realized my outdated approaches as a leader that I no longer required, such as being rigid and overly commanding in order to get others to listen or follow my lead. While sports played a part in this, I was still able to identify that it was not needed throughout my entire day and all my relationships—because others already followed me as a leader, whether commanded, or not.

This was because I lead by example and performance. I knew it wouldn't be a straight narrow path, but I was determined to make conscious decisions and efforts to embrace new challenges and barriers. I set my sights on obtaining a higher education (PhD), embedding intentional practices that would lead me to my desired end goals, followed by consistent strategic practices that developed life-long habits.

The plan was beginning, but it did not end there.

Regardless of the many barriers and pivots I had to make, as anyone else needs to do, my plan was completed when I shifted from reaction to reflection, from emotional decisions to grounded and aligned decisions, from check of the box approaches to questioning if this moves me forward or creates motion with no real movement towards my **[P]**lans. Each internal systems adjustment could not be accomplished in a moment's decision. I could embark on taking steps for that plan over the next decade, but together with strategy as my foundation and **[P]**lanning as my driver, I took action, which paved the way for my plan to become my future.

At this point in my life journey, I am now a seasoned young adult, tackling life with ease because I was able to pivot when hard times showed up.

I was now at a life-altering time in my life where I wanted to see what else was possible—How far can I actually go? Which means, it required me to pivot. I needed to go back to the **[S]**trategy and revise a new **[P]**lanning approach. As a working young adult, there were so many ways to turn. It was not easy; I hit roadblock after roadblock even with a plan in place. I had to dig much deeper and create smaller steps that were easier to win, so I did just that. I took my larger plan and narrowed it down even further. This is why it is so important to slow down before moving forward, especially when you begin to feel overwhelmed, alone, and just completely lost as though there is no end in sight.

Once I could see the end I had in mind for myself, I could map the steps in reverse. My method went beyond traditional project planning. I embarked on a journey of transformation. Instead of just identifying only what needed to be done, I identified what mindsets I owned, which mindsets needed to be fundamentally changed about how I would move forward in my life and what internal systems I need to support those changes.

That's why I say that effective and intentional **[P]**lanning is strategic backtracking. From personal growth to organizational goals, we use it as a way to build a bridge from where we are to where we want to be. How? By identifying which internal systems, processes, and approaches need to be updated or replaced, and redesigning transitional pathways that honor both stability and growth.

For me, the internal systems that needed to be challenged were my personal beliefs, perceived barriers, what support did I currently have or not have, and the professional goals I set out for myself. The turning point occurred when I switched from seeing my obstacles as "barriers" versus "hurdles." Instead of being frustrated that I was facing an obstacle that I saw as "holding me back," I chose to create a **[P]**lan to overcome it. And when I faced boulders that I could not change or lacked any input on, I chose to recognize where I could pivot and selected a different solution.

I can say with confidence that this mindset is what allowed me to not only become the first multiracial female on a SWAT team but also leave the police force after a mere two years on the force in order to pursue a higher income in the consulting space and thrive there to this day. My plan rooted me in a way that allowed me to create impact as an Industrial and Organizational Psychologist for other corporate leaders, professionals, coaches, and consultants.

I do not believe that such achievements are only mine to discover. Each of us can carve our own path as the multifaceted humans we are today! To begin, let's explore common mindset traps and how the right plan can help us overcome them.

Here is a quick S.P.A.R.K. Snapshot™ to help us determine what mindset to ditch and what to adopt:

Mindset to ditch	What it sounds like in your head	Mindset to adopt instead	New empowering truth
"Don't create waves."	If I speak up, I'll be seen as difficult. It's safer to stay quiet and go along with current norms.	**"My voice is meant to create change."**	Respectful disruption *is* leadership. Your perspective is not a problem to manage; it's a contribution others need.
"I'm the first ______. Therefore, I can't mess this up." (To graduate, to lead, to earn more, etc.)	If I fail, I'll let them down. I must prove I deserve to be here 24/7.	**"I'm the first, not the last."**	Being first means you're building a path, not embodying perfection. Your courage to go first makes it easier for others to follow.
"Who am I to lead/speak/ step up?"	I'm not experienced enough. Others know more than I do. I should wait until I'm "ready."	**"Who am I to *not* act?"**	Your lived experience is data. Your story, skills, and scars qualify you to lead right where you are right now, not later.
"I have to do it all alone."	If I ask for help, I'll look weak. No one else will get it right, therefore I must work extra to get it done.	**"Support is a strategy, not a weakness."**	Collaboration is how leaders scale impact. Asking for help is how you protect your energy, excellence, and longevity.
"If I slow down, I'll fall behind."	I can't rest; I'll lose my edge. I don't have time to pause and think.	**"If I ground myself, I rise stronger."**	Slowing down to reflect, reset, and realign gives you better decisions, clearer strategy, and sustainable success—both personally and professionally.

Mindset to ditch	What it sounds like in your head	Mindset to adopt instead	New empowering truth
"My role/title defines my worth."	If I lose this job or title, who am I? I need a bigger title to matter.	**"My worth is bigger than any title."**	Your title is a tool, not your identity. When you know who you are, roles and seasons can change without threatening your perceived value.
"I should be grateful and not want more."	People like me don't get this far. Asking for more is greedy or ungrateful.	**"Gratitude and growth can coexist."**	You can be deeply grateful and still climb higher. Wanting more alignment, impact, and wholeness is not selfish—it's stewardship of your potential.

In case you are thinking, "This sounds so simple and easy," I want to be clear. My own experience proves that living this type of mindset shift was far from easy. It is one thing to write on paper. It is another to live out in numerous environments. I have come to find out that there is no such thing as "perfect," either personally or professionally. Choosing to live out these crucial changes that I planned for myself meant I had to live out truth each time I faced "barriers" and "hurdles." You know the saying, "If it was easy, everyone would do it." It is not easy to adopt a new mindset. That is what makes us exceptional leaders who, in fact, are not everyone. We each get to steward our unique journey.

As you begin, consider taking time to look at the "hurdles" you face and what **F.E.A.R.** (False, Evidence, Appearing, Real) you feel. Then determine if the right reframe can help guide your plan as you ignite your **S.P.A.R.K.** on the table guide below:

Hurdle / Fear	Feels like	Helpful reframe	First step to try
"What if I try and fail?"	Fear of embarrassment, letting others down, or proving the inner critic "right."	Failure isn't proof you're not capable; it's proof you're *in motion*. Every leader you admire has failed but tried again many times.	Choose one small action that feels slightly uncomfortable but not overwhelming. Afterwards, write down what you learned, versus anything that went wrong. Process the learning with a trusted friend or loved one.

Hurdle / Fear	Feels like	Helpful reframe	First step to try
"What if I speak up and my team shuts me down?"	Dread that you'll be perceived as difficult, dramatic, or "too much."	No one's reaction can cancel your perspective. Resistance reveals their discomfort towards change, not your value.	Initiate one conversation in a **small, safe setting** (1:1 or with an ally). Present your feedback with a neutral tone: "Here's something I have noticed and why I care about it."
"What if I push for change and leaders don't listen?"	Powerlessness, invisibility, or that "it's not my place to question others."	Being ignored doesn't indicate you are in the wrong. It could mean the system is not ready yet. Even so, your clarity matters.	Document your findings (patterns, impact, risks). Share your observations with one leader you trust and ask, "Can we explore this together?" If you are told, "Not now." ask, "When would be a better time?"
"What if I lose motivation halfway through?"	Excitement at the start, followed by drain or discouragement when progress grinds to a halt.	Motivation comes and goes; **commitment** is what carries you. You don't need to feel inspired every day to remain moving forward.	Break your goal into **tiny, clear steps**. Pick one "10-minute win" you can accomplish today. Then, celebrate completion versus perfection.
"I don't know where to start."	Overwhelm, analysis paralysis, or waiting for the "perfect" plan to emerge before acting.	You don't need the full map to take the first step. Clarity often surfaces **after** you take action, not before.	Ask: "What is the smallest, most meaningful step I *do* know how to take?" Do that. Then determine the next step once more. Repeat. Aim for the *best next step* not your "forever plan."
"How can I even begin? My life is already full."	Overwhelm. The perception is there's no time, space, or energy to change, practically, emotionally, or mentally.	You don't have to alter your whole life. Small shifts in how you think, speak, or schedule can create huge ripple effects.	Choose **one area** (sleep, boundaries, saying no, asking for help) and make *one* small change this week. For example: "I will leave work 15 minutes earlier on one day," or "I will say no to one extra commitment."

Hurdle / Fear	Feels like	Helpful reframe	First step to try
"What if I outgrow people or make others uncomfortable?"	Fear of being perceived as "too ambitious," "too different," or "too much" by your current circle.	Your growth doesn't reject your roots; it expands what's possible for you *and* for those watching you.	Notice who supports your growth and who shames it. Spend a little more time with the people who celebrate your evolution.
"I don't know how to be more self-aware."	Confusion stemming from your own behaviors. Not fully understanding *why* you do *what* you do.	Awareness isn't rooted in judging yourself; it's an invitation to be curious about your patterns, learn from them, and be self-empowered to choose differently.	At the end of each day, ask yourself: "When did I feel most like myself today? When did I feel least like myself?" Write one sentence for each. That's your starting data.

You will face hurdles. That's guaranteed. What matters is not whether they show up, but whether you treat them as a stop sign or a signal like a yellow flashing light. It is okay to acknowledge them and then proceed with observed caution. When you view these challenges as signals instead of barriers, you are able to respond with intention, not fear, and keep rising, personally and professionally.

Dr. Patricia Williams, Chief Medical Officer at a major healthcare system, chose to see the obstacles in her way as signals versus stop signs. It was not easy. She faced the challenge of implementing new patient care protocols while maintaining quality and staff morale—all without halting the care of thousands that relied on her team to support their health on a day-to-day basis.

When it comes to planning, traditional healthcare approaches suggest top-down implementation and the use of standardized training modules. Patricia, however, recognized that this approach had failed repeatedly. Why? Because healthcare settings tend to ignore the complex human dynamics which are present in medical decision-making.

Patricia didn't just create a rollout schedule; she designed a system-wide approach to transform the norm at a root level. She started with the end vision. She sought to provide excellent patient care that integrated advanced technology with personalized human attention. Working backward from this vision, she identified which protocols were currently creating barriers to that vision and what culture patterns needed to shift for that vision to become reality. Her planning process included physician input at every stage, phased implementation that allowed for real-time adjustments, and integrated AI tools that enhanced versus replaced clinical judgment.

The results her team accomplished defied typical healthcare implementation timelines. Instead of facing the usual 18-month struggle, complete with resistance and inconsistent adoption, Patricia's approach achieved full integration in eight months. On top of this, they achieved 95% staff satisfaction and measurably improved patient outcomes. She proved that planning for systematic transformation, rather than just procedural change, creates both faster adoption and better results.

How did she do it? Patricia planned well as she:

- **Defined the end goal**. This gave her a benchmark to examine what current systems or approaches were incompatible with that goal.
- Identified the necessary steps she would have to take to see the vision come to pass. This included selecting which outdated processes need to be replaced or updated.
- **Determined the tools, resources, and internal systems** that must be introduced to support the change. Additionally, she had to ensure each one would integrate technological efficiency with human-centered values.
- **Asked**: *Who can help me—and who may be holding me back?* She addressed resistance that was rooted in any single team member's attachment to outdated approaches.
- **Focused on solutions**, not problems. Through the transformation process, she recognized that what looked like "problems" were often symptoms of systems that needed updating.

Dr. Patricia's story shows that planning isn't about building a prettier timeline; it's about designing a path that honors both the humans and the outcomes. She didn't just ask, "How fast can we roll this out?" She asked, "What kind of care are we committed to, and what kind of internal system do we need to get there?" That's the difference between procedural change and internal systems transformation. The good news is each of us has an ability to plan this way. You can use the same **[P]**lanning lens in your role, your team, your business, and even your personal life.

<u>Planning Step</u>	<u>What this means</u>	<u>Questions to consider</u>	<u>Your notes / examples</u>
1. Define the end goal	Start with a vision of what "better" actually looks like. What does it look like personally, professionally, or organizationally?	• What is the outcome I/we truly want? • How will people feel, work, or live differently when the vision is in place? • What current systems or approaches are incompatible with that goal?	

<u>Planning Step</u>	<u>What this means</u>	<u>Questions to consider</u>	<u>Your notes / examples</u>
2. Identify the steps and outdated pieces	Work backward from the vision in mind and map the key steps it will take to achieve it. Notice what processes, habits, or patterns do not belong.	• What shifts must occur to reach this vision? • What processes need to be updated, simplified, or removed? • When do we plateau "because we have always done it that way?"	——————— ——————— ——————— ———————
3. Determine tools, resources, and systems	Decide what support you need—people, tools, and systems. Make sure that anything introduced is present to help humans, not replace them.	• What tools, resources, or systems would make it easier and more effective to reach the goal? • How can we integrate technological efficiency while staying human-centered? • What do we need to stop using because it no longer serves us?	——————— ——————— ———————
4. Identify support and resistance	Get honest about who will help and who might resist upcoming changes—and why.	• Who can help champion this change? • Who might feel threatened, left out, or attached to the old way? • How can I address resistance without indicating shame, but instead be a source of support?	——————— ——————— ———————
5. Stay solution centered	Treat recurring problems as signals that systems need upgraded. Refuse to view this as evidence of failure.	• What problems keep repeating, no matter who is in the role? • If this is a symptom, what system might be causing it? • What is one solution-focused action I can take this week to move us forward?	——————— ——————— ——————— ———————

When you plan by starting at the end, working backward, and honoring both people and internal systems—you stop "winging it." Instead, you are empowered to walk a path that is designed for the future you envision.

I do not believe there is ever a time when there is no solution. When challenges come, we must study them, learn from them, and adjust accordingly. Many times, these obstacles serve as feedback which signal an outdated approach that must be replaced with a more effective alternative.

This is the exact mindset I use that has shaped how I lead both personally and professionally. It's also how I come alongside others, equipping them to rise with progress, not perfection. Over and over, as an Industrial and Organizational Psychologist, I have come to see that it is only by strategically driven **[P]**lanning and approaches, that honor both individual authenticity and organizational effectiveness, that leadership can truly emerge and business goals can be intentionally obtained.

What happens when you are tasked with creating change, versus when it stems from your own vision?

Consider Michael Chen, a senior finance director at a global investment firm. He was given the responsibility of modernizing his company's risk assessment processes. The traditional approach would have been to upgrade existing software and retrain staff on new procedures. Michael, however, wanted to create something that would last. He recognized that risk assessment training was traditionally based on market assumptions and siloed decision-making structures versus human needs.

Instead of planning a software upgrade, Michael saw the opportunity to plan for transformation. His end vision? He imagined his organization could provide risk assessments that combined AI-powered data analysis with human expertise and cross-functional collaboration. Working backward from this vision, he identified what silos needed to be dissolved, what communication channels needed to be updated, and which decision-making norms had created blind spots.

Michael's planning process included stakeholder alignment sessions, phased technology integration, cultural change management, and continuous feedback loops. The transformation didn't just improve their risk assessment accuracy; it also created a model of collaborative decision-making. In time, other departments were able to adopt his learnings into their operations. Michael proved that planning for internal systematic change, rather than just procedural updates, creates ripple effects that strengthen entire organizations.

Just like Patricia and Michael, this is your moment to plan with intentional purpose. You have what it takes to build a roadmap that makes your vision real, not just on paper, but in your day-to-day life. In turn, this has the power to deepen your professional leadership.

Many of us know that as soon as we create a plan, it will need to change. New information and evolving dynamics require us to pivot while remaining anchored in our strategy. To help us bend and not break, we must choose a mindset of adaptability which is built through intentional rhythms, not random reactions. To help us with that, let's consider what processes allow us to make such a shift.

That might look like:

Adaptability Process	What it looks like	How it helps you
Regular check-ins/ retros	Weekly or monthly planned pauses to review what's working, what's not, and what needs to change.	The pause keeps you from drifting. You adjust early instead of waiting for a crisis.
Short planning cycles	30–90-day plans instead of rigid 12-month ones.	Short plans provide room to pivot while still moving toward your long-term vision.
Feedback loops	Asking team members, clients, or stakeholders for honest input regularly.	Feedback surfaces blind spots and opportunities you can't see alone.
Scenario planning	Exploring "If X happens, how would we respond?" in advance.	Scenario planning reduces panic when change comes. You've already thought through pivot options.
Flexible systems	Processes built with options, versus one standard way.	Options allow you to shift without starting over every time change occurs.

Let's dive into one last scenario to see how one CEO took these principles and put them in action.

[P]lanning: The Core Approach

Scenario: A rapidly growing company is expanding into new markets but lacks a consistent approach across its departments. Trent, who serves as CEO, wants to improve alignment, reduce confusion, and prepare for sustainable scale. The only problem? He doesn't know where to begin. After all, getting multiple department heads to align is not easy.

Traditional expansion planning tends to focus on hiring plans, market analysis, and resource allocation. Many of these are important and necessary. But Trent knows that his fundamental challenge isn't capacity or logistics; it's the absence of organizational coherence that supports their rapid growth.

Here is what Trent knows. It is not that traditional planning is wrong. Instead, it tends to be a stand-alone idea. It doesn't ensure that his company will collectively grow in the same direction and towards the same purpose.

S.P.A.R.K. Framework™ – Planning Solution:

Using **[P]**lanning, Trent invited his leadership team to boldly state their desired future state. Together, they determined that they wanted to expand operations and include clearly defined roles, systems, and decision-making power. By doing so, they went beyond solely planning operational expansion. Trent hosted conversations, which allowed his team to plan for a system-wide transformation that ensured their organizational culture and values would remain intact while the structure evolved.

They worked backward from this vision. Key initiatives included identifying key hires, clarifying standard operating procedures, and using tech to outline a 90-day and 12-month plan. Each part of the plan ensured strategic clarity at every level. Most importantly, they discovered which current approaches allowed inconsistency between departments. They updated their processes to replace ad hoc decision-making with values-aligned choices instead.

To reduce overwhelm, they took their planning process one step further to integrate AI tools to take on the load when it came to project coordination and performance tracking. But the tools did not outrank the humans who ran each department. They only adopted tech functions which preserved human judgment for strategic decisions and relationship management. These adaptive frameworks, in turn, accommodated the rapid growth they faced while maintaining a collaborative culture that was a key driver to their innovation.

For Trent, planning unfolded through our Obstacle → Opportunity → Option → Outcome flow, with **[P]**lanning as the anchor.

	<u>What Was Happening</u>	<u>Option ([P]lanning Approach)</u>	<u>What Happened as a Result</u>
Obstacle	A rapidly growing company is expanding into new markets but lacks a consistent approach across departments. The CEO wants alignment, clarity, and sustainable scale but doesn't know where to begin. Traditional expansion planning would focus on hiring plans, market analysis, and resource allocation—important, but incomplete on their own.	We named the real issue: Their fundamental challenge wasn't just capacity or logistic—it was the **absence of internal systems and approaches** that could maintain organizational coherence while the business grew quickly.	Without a different kind of plan, growth would continue to magnify confusion, inconsistency, and misalignment as more people and markets were added.
Opportunity	The tension between rapid growth and internal confusion created a turning point: Keep or use	The CEO chose to see growth as an opportunity to plan for **systematic transformation**, not just	This shift opened the door to building a business that could scale without losing

	What Was Happening	**Option ([P]lanning Approach)**	**What Happened as a Result**
	this moment to design a cohesive way of operating.	operational expansion, so that culture, values, and structure could grow together.	its identity or burning out its people.
Option (Our [P]lanning Approach)	Old planning = "How do we add more?" New planning = "How do we grow in a way that remains clear in communication, aligned, and human-centered?"	Using **[P]**lanning, the leadership team: • Mapped their **desired future state**: expanded operations with clearly defined roles, systems, and decision-making power, so everyone knew what "good" looked like. • Worked **backward from the vision**, identifying key hires, standard operating procedures, and technology needed, outlining both a 90-day and 12-month plan to ensure strategic clarity at every level. • Identified which current approaches were creating inconsistency and designed **transitional strategies** to replace ad hoc decision-making with systematic, values-aligned processes. • Integrated **AI tools** for project coordination and performance tracking, while preserving human judgment for strategic decisions and relationship management. • Created **adaptive frameworks** that could flex with rapid growth while protecting the collaborative culture that made them innovative.	Planning became a living blueprint, not a static document, one that guided how they hired, communicated, made decisions, and used tools as they scaled.

	What Was Happening	**Option ([P]lanning Approach)**	**What Happened as a Result**
Outcome	Before, growth meant more confusion and misalignment.	After, they experienced **momentum with structure and growth with direction**. The business scaled with intention, not chaos.	They created a model of **systematic expansion** that maintained organizational integrity while achieving operational excellence—proving that planning for transformation, not just growth, creates sustainable competitive advantage.

Trent's example shows us what **[P]**lanning looks like when it moves beyond dates and deadlines and creates a unique blueprint to design collective growth while keeping other humans in mind. Instead of asking, "How fast can we expand and increase profits?" this leadership team dared to ask, "How do we expand in a way that keeps us clear in our communication, while remaining aligned in both our values and bottom-line goals and remaining human-centered in our approach?"

By answering that question, Trent discovered the power of planning for transformation, versus only valuing profit. As a result, he didn't just build a bigger business, his team built a stronger one. No matter your role, the size of your team, your title, or the current chapter of your life, this same approach is available to you.

To break it down using your personal and professional lens, I would like to invite you to reflect, plan, and prepare to take action. Let's bring planning to life with your own experience.

[P]lanning For Organizations and Teams

Operational Planning for Growth

What are your top three organizational priorities for the next 12 months?

____

____

What current systems or processes might be creating barriers to achieving these priorities?

____

____

How can you ensure alignment between departments, leaders, and teams?

____

____

What outdated communication or decision-making structures need to be updated to support this alignment?

____

____

What systems, processes, or policies need to be created or improved?

____

____

How can you integrate technological efficiency and human-centered approaches into these systems?

____

____

What potential roadblocks or resistance might surface—and how will you address them?

____

____

Which resistance do you believe you might face? How much of it could be rooted in attachment to outdated approaches? How might you create safe transitions to more effective alternatives?

____

____

How will you track progress, celebrate wins, and refine your plan as needed?

____

____

How will you ensure your tracking measures both operational outcomes and organizational health?

____

____

For Leaders

Executive-Level Planning for Influence

What legacy do you want to leave behind?

____

____

What outdated leadership approaches do you need to release in order to create this legacy?

____

____

What daily habits or routines can you begin to remain focused on this legacy?

____

____

How do these habits model the systematic, intentional approaches you want to see throughout your organization?

____

____

What do you need to delegate or entrust to your team?

____

____

What systems or processes do you need to implement to ensure effective delegation while maintaining strategic alignment?

____

____

How can you support individual team member growth while driving collective outcomes?

____

____

How does an individualistic approach replace traditional performance management?

____

____

What systems or scorecards will you use to measure your leadership success?

____

____

How will you measure both quantitative outcomes and qualitative cultural indicators?

____

____

For Coaches and Consultants

Business Planning for Sustainable Impact

What services or offerings do you want to be known for one year from now?

____

____

What scattered or unfocused approaches do you need to phase out to achieve this goal?

What is your ideal client volume or revenue milestone? What date are you seeking to achieve this by?

How does planning prioritize your sustainable impact over unsustainable scaling?

What content, systems, or backend tools do you need to streamline your service delivery?

What systems can you use to integrate AI efficiency with human connection to create authentic transformation?

What partnerships, platforms, or marketing strategies can support this growth?

Which of these strategies align with your authentic expertise rather than generic industry trends?

What mindset or belief do you need to shift to execute your services consistently?

____

____

What approach will you implement to support a mindset shift rather than relying on willpower alone?

____

____

For Individuals

Personal Planning for Intentional Living

What personal goal do you want to accomplish in the next 90 days?

____

____

What outdated beliefs about achievement or success have created unnecessary obstacles to your goal?

____

____

What daily habits or routines support that outcome?

____

____

What scattered activity needs to be replaced with focused, intentional progress?

____

____

Who in your life can support your journey?

____

____

Who do you need to set boundaries with?

____

____

How will you communicate these boundaries in ways that honor your growth and your relationships?

____

____

What will progress look like 30, 60, and 90 days from now?

____

____

How will you measure external achievements?

____

____

How will you measure internal transformation?

____

____

What reward or celebration will you give yourself when you hit your first milestone?

____

____

How does this celebration reflect your authentic values versus seeking external validation?

____

____

Here is what I know: You don't need flawless plans.

You simply need a committed one. More important than that, you need adaptability to evolve with changing circumstances while maintaining strategic direction. **[P]**lanning is the step where your vision becomes a visible path. It is where internal systematic transformation replaces outdated approaches with sustainable alternatives. In turn, this supports the humans you care for, both your internal teams and external consumer base.

Such change has the power to last beyond any single project, initiative, or go-to market strategy. Your legacy is fueled by human service and leadership that exhibits deep care.

This is what **[P]**lanning looks like in the real world—committed, clear, and courageous enough to evolve as you do.

Quote to Close the Chapter:

You don't need more time—you need more alignment. With alignment, movement is inevitable. Paired with systematic planning, transformation becomes sustainable.

— Dr. Michelle Brown

Next Up – Chapter 6 [A]ction: Align, Activate, Advance!

You've clarified your **[S]**trategy and mapped your **[P]**lanning. You've named what needs to change and began to see the kind of future you're called to build. But vision and plans—even powerful ones—don't transform anything on their own.

The real shift happens when you start moving.

In Chapter 6, we'll step into the gap where many quietly stall. We will move past the space of *knowing* and step into *doing*. We'll talk honestly about fear, overthinking, perfectionism, and "sophisticated procrastination" that looks productive but keeps you safely stuck. We'll replace it with aligned, courageous **[A]**ction—finding small, consistent steps that challenge comfortable internal systems and patterns; and build sustainable alternatives instead.

You'll see how leaders used **[A]**ction to redefine entire internal systems, not just tweak them. You'll be guided through prompts so you can decide: What action am I willing to take next to move into the future I say I want?

Discover how your strategy and planning can stop living as theory and start becoming your new reality—one aligned, imperfect, powerful action at a time.

CHAPTER 6 – [A]CTION
ALIGN, ACTIVATE, ADVANCE!

Thus far in our journey, you've defined your **[S]**trategy and mapped out your **[P]**lanning. Now, it's time to generate momentum through **[A]**ction, because without it, vision is stuck on paper and transformation remains a distant dream, not reality. **[A]**ction is where purpose meets motion and clarity becomes courage.

Here's what conventional advice misses: Most "action" is sophisticated procrastination disguised as productivity. There may be motion, but it is rarely in the direction of true transformation. Changes feel progressive but leaves fundamental internal systems untouched.

In short: We are extremely busy—but unwilling to disrupt what no longer works.

How does this play out in our organizations? It looks like rebranding instead of rethinking, rearranging instead of rebuilding, and adding onto a broken foundation instead of pausing to repair what's underneath. Such "action" keeps everyone in motion, but very little changes and leaders wonder why.

Wonder if you are facing sophisticated procrastination? See if you recognize its tune. It sounds like:

- "Let's roll out another training," instead of asking, *"Why does this behavior keep repeating in the first place?"*
- "Let's launch a new initiative," instead of examining, *"Which of our current internal systems are quietly working against our goals?"*
- "Let's add another tool or platform," instead of facing the reality that, *"Our processes and decision-making are so unclear that no tool can fix this."*

How does sophisticated procrastination sound on an individual level? It sounds like:

1. Color-coding your day planner instead of committing to take one step.

2. Enrolling in one more course, certification, or mastermind instead of proceeding on what you already know.

3. Constantly "preparing" for change by researching, brainstorming, and vision-boarding—all without making a decision that disrupts your comfort.

These activities *feel* like action because it's stuff to do, but the same patterns resurface each time. They do not eradicate organizational culture problems, communication gaps, or high turnover rates. There is still misalignment between what's said and what's done—or not done.

Sophisticated procrastination means the:

- Activity level is high.
- Impact on core internal systems is low.
- Patterns don't change.
- Conversations stay the same month after month

Transformational action, however, is different.

Transformational action asks, *"What needs to shift in our beliefs, decisions, structures, and internal systems for this change to stick?"* Then it moves—imperfectly and courageously—in that direction. How? Through informed action steps.

To accomplish this, you may need to:

- Change who is in the room when decisions are made.
- Redesign how performance is measured, rewarded, and developed.
- Update internal systems with informed AI integrations, so that what you say you value is actually how you operate.
- Say no to "busy" projects that look impressive, but don't move the mission or help the humans you serve.

Here is the core difference between taking action and using **[A]**ction from the **S.P.A.R.K. Framework™**:

Saying no to **more** action. Saying yes to **true intentional** actions.

Passing up **louder** movement. Moving towards **deeper** change.

Recognizing that **effort** that keeps you safe, but **action** shifts internal systems and outcomes.

To help you spot the difference, let's unpack commons sayings, and what is hiding behind them:

When it looks like action…	What it really is… (Sophisticated Procrastination)	What transformational action looks like instead…
"We launched a new initiative."	This looks like a fresh project layered on top of the same outdated systems. The root issues are untouched.	Instead, pause to ask, *"What internal system created this problem?"* Next, you redesign that internal system before your next initiative.
"We rolled out another training."	This only teaches people how to survive in a broken environment versus fixing the environment itself.	Instead, address the policies, incentives, organizational culture, and expectations that drive behavior first. This allows training to factor in who your unique professionals are and what they need. Change can flow from this grounded perspective versus over-compensating with generic training.
"We bought a new tool/technology."	This only speeds up confusion. It amplifies unclear processes, making mistakes faster and fixing them more expensive.	Instead, clarify the process and decision-making first, then choose tools that support that clarity. The goal is to free humans for higher-value work.
"We had a lot of meetings about it."	Time spent talking in circles, revisiting the same issues, means we are only avoiding hard decisions.	Instead, meetings end with clear decisions, owners, and next steps that outline how work happens. Progress is visible and trackable.
"I made a new plan/spreadsheet/to-do list."	Personal planning only delays the first uncomfortable step. It feels productive but changes nothing.	Instead, choose one aligned, uncomfortable action and do it, even while the plan is still imperfect. You refine the action as you move forward.
"I signed up for another course/program."	This is an indication of endless preparation. Learning more is a way to avoid acting on what you already know.	Instead, implement one concept you've already learned, test it in real life, and let experience teach you the next adjustment.
"We're really busy."	This indicates there is high motion, low impact. The same internal problems keep repeating.	Instead, point to specific shifts in internal systems, behaviors, or outcomes and say, *"This is different now and here's how we know."*

If the work does not change the internal systems that create results, this means it's simply **sophisticated procrastination.**

[A]ction is where that changes.

Real action isn't about doing more—it's about doing what fundamentally shifts the internal systems that create real results. It's about having the courage to stop accepting "how things have always been done" and start creating "how things could and should be done."

But here's the truth: Many people stall here. This is not because they lack ideas. It is because they fear taking the wrong step or are consumed with overwhelm. But do you know what I think? I believe that what they're really afraid of isn't failure. Instead, they're afraid of success that would require them to operate at a level that challenges every comfortable pattern they've developed over the span of their lifetime.

So, what happens instead? They wait, overthink, and hesitate. What started as **[P]**lanning quickly turns into paralysis.

Now, let me be clear: **F.E.A.R.** is a very real thing, but it's also **False Evidence Appearing Real**. The "evidence" is often an attachment to a standard way of doing something. It feels familiar, but is the very thing limiting your potential.

I want you to know: You don't need a perfect start. You just need to start and do it. You need to take action that challenges the status quo while building sustainable alternatives. You need to move beyond your comfort zone and into your transformation zone.

This is exactly why I started Brown Transformations Consulting. Repeatedly, I heard from leaders who didn't need more ideas—they needed a clear, supported way to create new ways of working, leading, and deciding. Time and time again, I have watched individuals embrace the gap between *"we know this has to change"* and *"this is how we will act to change it in our internal systems, day by day."* This kind of **[A]**ction matters most when it's uncomfortable, when it stretches your patterns, and when it challenges everything you thought you knew about how things "should" work.

[A]ction is rooted in finding a solution that fits your alignment. This should line up with:

- **Your values** — what matters most and is non-negotiable.
- **Your needs** — your real capacity, support, wellbeing, and constraints.
- **Your tech opportunities** — where internal systems, tools, and AI can carry the load so humans can focus on what only humans can do.

This level of alignment must bridge the divide between individual authenticity and organizational effectiveness, technological efficiency and human-centered values, immediate needs and long-term transformation.

To make this practical, consider taking a quick alignment check—first personally, then professionally:

Personally: Your Action Alignment Check

Instead of only asking, *"What do I need to do?"*, pause and ask:

1) **Values – "Is this option I am considering acting on true to who I am?"**

    a. Does this action move me closer to the end goal I have for myself and the life I'm building?
    b. Does it reflect the kind of leader, parent, partner, and human I want and need to be?

2) **Needs – "Is this option I am considering acting on sustainable for me?"**

    a. Do I have the time, energy, and support to do this well right now?
    b. What boundaries or adjustments do I need so this doesn't drain me past empty?

3) **Tech & Systems – "What can I systematize or streamline?"**

    a. Is there a tool, template, workflow, or AI support that could simplify this option?
    b. What part of this option truly requires *me*, versus what could be supported by an internal system?

If an action honors your values, respects your needs, and uses tech or internal systems wisely—you're not just doing more, you're doing what's *aligned*.

Professionally: Your Action Alignment Check

At work, don't just ask, *"What decision should we make?"* Ask:

- **Values – "Does this option we are considering acting on reflect who we say we are?"**

    o Does this option move the organization closer to our desired end goal—or is it reactive?
    o Does this option still serve our clients' and consumers' needs, or does it only serve our bottom-line or ROI?

- **Needs – "Is this option we are considering acting on realistic and responsible?"**

    o Do our teams have the capacity, skills, and support to carry this option out?
    o What do we need to say *no* to in order to do this well?

- **Tech & Systems – "What internal systems need to shift in order to fully utilize this option?"**

    o Are we implementing changes that look progressive but allow fundamental systems to remain untouched?

    o What technology or AI tools can help streamline workflows, decisions, or communication, without replacing human judgment or relationships?

You must do this to avoid paralysis and overthinking, because:

1. Being busy doesn't equal progress.
2. Motion doesn't equal movement.
3. Movement doesn't always indicate purposeful growth.
4. Comfortable action rarely equals transformational action.

[A]ction is not about doing everything. It's about doing the right next thing. It allows us to take decisive, aligned, and continuous action, especially when it's imperfect. Often, it challenges internal systems everyone else accepts as "just how things are."

Consider the transformation of Dr. James Rodriguez, President of a major state university. He faced declining enrollment, outdated curricula, and faculty-wide resistance to change. Traditionally universities create action plans that focus on marketing campaigns and minor program updates. Essentially, this comes down to rearranging deck chairs while ignoring fundamental shifts in how education must function in our technological age.

Dr. Rodriguez recognized that the challenges he faced weren't marketing problems or budget problems. They were internal system problems that required him to ignite a systematic transformation. Instead of comfortable, incremental changes, he took bold action that would fundamentally reimagine higher education delivery to his students.

Dr. Rodriguez didn't just implement new programs; he changed how the university approached education, career preparation, and community engagement. Action meant replacing lecture-heavy curricula with experiential learning models, integrating AI-powered personalized education paths while maintaining human mentorship. It also inspired him to create industry partnerships that made education immediately applicable to career success.

The results were revolutionary. Within two years, enrollment increased by 35%. Student satisfaction reached record highs. Employers actively recruited their graduates. More importantly, other universities began studying their transformation model and adopted similar actions into their foundation. Dr. Rodriguez proved that when leaders are willing to take action that challenges fundamental assumptions, they don't just solve problems—they redefine entire industries.

Dr. Rodriguez faced an obstacle, which led to opportunity, which became an option, which created a desired outcome—all which kept [A]ction at the center.

<u>**Summary**</u>

Obstacle	As President of a major state university, Dr. Rodriguez was facing declining enrollment, outdated curricula, and faculty resistance to change. Most "action plans" were surface-level—more marketing, small program tweaks—while the entire model of higher education was shifting around them.
Opportunity	Instead of treating this as a marketing or budget problem, he named the real issue: Their internal systems for how education was designed, delivered, and connected to real careers no longer matched the world students were graduating into. That realization turned a crisis into a chance to lead, not just keep up.
[A]ction – What He Did Differently	Using the **S.P.A.R.K. Framework™** with **[A]**ction at the center, he: (1) replaced lecture-heavy curricula with experiential learning; (2) integrated AI-powered personalized learning paths while keeping human mentorship; and (3) built industry partnerships so students could clearly see the path from classroom to career. Every move was designed to upgrade internal systems, not just launch one-off projects.
Outcome	Within two years, enrollment increased, student satisfaction hit new highs, and employers actively sought their graduates. Other universities began studying their model as a roadmap for the future. Dr. Rodriguez proved that when leaders take **[A]**ction that challenges assumptions and transforms internal systems, they don't just fix problems—they redefine what's possible for an entire industry.

Dr. Rodriguez's story reminds us that **[A]**ction isn't about doing more, it's about doing what *truly* moves us into new internal systems, even when it feels bold, different, or uncomfortable.

When Change Feels Too Big (or Too Risky)

Let's be honest: Challenging outdated internal systems, pushing past comfortable patterns, and initiating real transformation sounds powerful on paper, but can feel terrifying and overwhelming in real life.

You might be thinking:

1. *"This takes buy-in from stakeholders who don't want to change."*
2. *"If I push for this, it might look like a power play."*
3. *"I don't have enough authority or clout to influence systems."*
4. *"I'm introverted. I don't want to be the loudest voice in the room."*
5. *"What if there really is no solution here?"*
6. *"What if what I suggest, fails?"*

If you have felt these ringing in the back of your head, you're not doing anything wrong—you're simply human.

My goal isn't to ignore those fears; it's to acknowledge them in a grounded way. You don't have to be the CEO, the loudest voice, or the one with all the power to spark change. You simply must start where you *do* have influence. Many times, this is in your mindset, your conversations, your corner of the internal system, and *your* next action.

If [A]ction feels risky, consider working through how to maneuver the following thoughts:

	What it really means	**How to move through it**	**Questions to use which invite curiosity**
"I don't have enough power to change anything."	You see the problem but are doubting your influence because you're not "at the top."	Start with your sphere of influence—in your role, your team, and your projects. Systemic change often starts with proof-of-concept in one small area.	"In one project, could my team test a different way of doing this for 30 days and then we could meet to discuss the results?"
"People here don't want to change."	There is real resistance. This is likely rooted in fear, fatigue, or past broken promises, versus stubbornness towards you alone.	Lead with curiosity, not confrontation. Ask questions. Listen to what people are afraid of losing and connect change to things they already care about.	"What worries you most about changing this process?" / "If this actually worked, what relief would it create in your day-to-day operations?"
"If I push for this, it will look like a power play."	You care about being respectful and don't want to be perceived as trying to take over.	Anchor your ideas in shared purpose, not personal agenda. Frame it as "we" and "our goals," not "my idea vs. theirs."	"I'm sharing because I think this option could help us serve our clients better and reduce stress on the team. Can we explore it together?"
"I'm introverted. I don't want to create waves."	You bring depth and insight but avoid speaking up in order to feel safe or remain unseen.	Use your strengths: Ask thoughtful questions. Seek one-on-one conversations. Use written communication. You don't have to be loud in a crowded room to be impactful.	"I've reflected on something I have noticed. Could I share a few thoughts in writing and get your feedback 1-1?"

	<u>What it really means</u>	<u>How to move through it</u>	<u>Questions to use which invite curiosity</u>
"What if there is no solution?"	You're tired, discouraged, or feel like you've tried everything	Shift from "solve everything" to "shift one thing." Look for one system, rule, or routine that *can* be adjusted and start there.	"We may not fix the whole system at once, but could we start by changing how we do X for this team/department and see what happens?"
"This will take everyone's buy-in—I can't get that."	You're imagining you need unanimous agreement before you move.	You don't need everyone to start; you need a small coalition. Find 1–3 allies who see what you see and co-create a small, safe experiment.	"I have heard you mentioned this challenge before. Could we meet to discuss what it would look like to pilot a new approach and share our results with leadership?"

When I see individuals shift their mindset and move towards curiosity, it gets me excited. I love seeing leaders and organizations move through the transition from outdated internal systems to sustainable alternatives. Through the expertise, support, and accountability our team provides, we have seen countless individuals take bold actions that creates lasting transformation rather than temporary changes.

Your Turn: When It Feels Like You Don't Have Power

You may not be able to flip an entire internal system overnight, but you are never powerless. Your influence lives within your sphere of influence, in your voice, in your approaches, and in your next aligned action step.

In case you are looking to ground yourself when you feel like there's no solution or you do not carry enough clout, consider working through this worksheet:

Step 1: Name Your Sphere of Influence

Change doesn't always start at the top. It starts where you are.

<u>Prompt</u>	**<u>Your reflection</u>**
Where do I have influence right now? **Think:** Consider your role, team, projects, clients, students, and circle.	
Who tends to listen when I speak up or share an idea? (*Even if it's just one person.*)	
What decisions do I already make, even if they feel small?	

Step 2: Identify One Internal Pattern or System You Can Touch

You don't have to fix the whole system. Start with one pattern.

<u>Prompt</u>	**<u>Your reflection</u>**
What one recurring issue do I keep seeing that bothers me?	
Is this really a "people problem," or is it an internal systems problem? (*A process, rule, habit, or unspoken norm.*)	
What one part of this internal system can I influence, make suggestions for, or model differently?	

Step 3: Choose One Aligned Action (Quiet, Courageous, and Realistic)

Remember, your power is in intentional, thoughtful action—not volume.

Prompt	**Your reflection**
What is one small, safe experiment I could suggest or launch in my sphere?	
Think: This might look like a new way to run a meeting, a different communication flow, a small pilot, or a new question to begin asking.	
Who could I invite as an ally or thought partner so I'm not acting on this alone?	
How can I express my vision in a way that centers our shared goals, not my ego or frustration? *Write a sentence you feel comfortable saying or writing in an email.*	
What does success look like for this small step?	
How will I know this action step made a difference?	

You may not be able to uproot every internal system or convince each stakeholder today, but through this exercise you have named where your real power lives. It is within your sphere, your patterns, and your next aligned step.

That's where transformation always begins.

One aligned action, one honest conversation, or one small experiment in your corner of the organization can become the proof that bigger change is needed and possible.

Sarah Mitchell, VP of Operations at a major oil and gas company, felt this pressure when it came to **[A]**ction. She faced the challenge of implementing sustainable practices while maintaining operational efficiency and profitability. Traditional action in this industry focuses on compliance, doing the minimum required to meet regulations while maintaining established extraction and processing methods.

However, Sarah recognized that their industry's future depended on fundamental transformation, not just regulatory compliance. She saw the need for larger scale change. Instead of taking comfortable action that maintained the status quo, she championed systematic changes that positioned their company as an industry leader in sustainable energy transition.

How did she do it? Sarah didn't just implement new policies, she transformed how her company approached resource development, community engagement, and long-term planning. Why? Because her values led her to believe this was the most important way to conduct business in the energy space. For her, **[A]**ction included investing in renewable energy integration, retraining workforce for emerging technologies, and creating transparent community partnership models that addressed environmental concerns proactively rather than reactively.

The transformation she ushered in defied industry expectations and their company became the preferred partner for communities and governments who, same as Sarah, sought responsible resource development. Employee retention improved dramatically as workers felt proud of their company's leadership. Stock performance outpaced competitors who remained stuck in traditional approaches. Sarah proved that taking action that challenges industry norms isn't "risky"—it's rooted in strategy, planning, and action, even if it goes against the "norm."

Sarah reminds us that in both life and leadership, action must be rooted in why we do something, not just what we are doing. But more than that **[A]**ction must be rooted in the courage to challenge norms that no longer serve us while building alternatives that actually do. This is how industries evolve and individuals become the leaders who redefine what's possible.

Sarah proved that taking **[A]**ction that challenges industry norms isn't risky—it's strategic.

<u>**Summary**</u>

Obstacle

As VP of Operations in a major oil and gas company, Sarah was under pressure to "be more sustainable" while keeping efficiency and profit high. In reality, most action was minimum compliance doing just enough to meet regulations and protect the old way of operating.

Opportunity

The growing gap between public expectations, regulatory pressure, and their old operating model became a wake-up call. Sarah recognized this wasn't just a compliance issue, it was a signal that their action playbook was built for a past that no longer existed.

Our Approach
[A]ction Shift

Instead of staying in checkbox mode, Sarah chose transformational action: investing in renewables alongside traditional operations, retraining the workforce for emerging technologies, and proactively partnering with communities to address environmental concerns.

Outcome

The company shifted from "reluctant follower" to preferred partner in responsible energy. Trust deepened, retention improved, and performance outpaced competitors who clung to the old model. Sarah proved that bold, values-aligned action isn't reckless, it's strategic.

Sarah went beyond doing more of the same. Her **[A]**ction was rooted in taking steps that matched the future she was committed to building, not the past she felt pressured to protect. She chose to release "how it's always been" and move toward "what we actually need now." And you can, too.

When you choose aligned **[A]**ction over automatic reaction, you stop rehearsing the old story and start writing a new one—one deliberate decision at a time.

Scenario: A leadership team is paralyzed by decision fatigue during a major company pivot. Fear of making the wrong move stalls progress. Employees are anxious and productivity dips.

Traditional approaches lean on crisis management, making quick decisions to reduce anxiety and restore familiar patterns, but this leadership team recognized that their paralysis was less about their ability to decide and more about a fundamental gap in their current decision-making process.

Using the **S.P.A.R.K. Framework™**, the **[A]**ction solution was: The leadership team revisited their **[S]**trategy and **[P]**lanning. In doing so, they identified one aligned action they could take within the next 30 days. The action they chose? They decided to launch a weekly town hall to be transparent and re-engage staff.

This initiative went beyond just communication. They replaced closed-door decision-making with transparency and collaboration. This proved to team members that leadership could navigate uncertainty effectively and that their feedback truly mattered.

This simple, people-centered step rebuilt trust and drove aligned momentum. More importantly, it modeled system-wide transparency that transformed organizational culture from the inside out. By creating adaptive internal systems, the entire organization got stronger under pressure rather than weaker.

Result: Confidence returned. Teams felt seen. Leaders took back control of the chaos, one aligned action at a time. More significantly, they created a model of crisis leadership that other organizations began to study and replicate. This proved that transformational [A]ction, even during challenges, can create competitive advantage rather than vulnerability.

Let's explore how you too can take aligned, sustainable action—both personally and professionally—with space to reflect and commit to your next move. Our goal is to move away from comfortable motion that maintains limitations and toward transformational action that creates breakthroughs.

[A]ction Section

For Organizations and Teams

From Motion to Meaningful Movement

What one initiative or project is currently stuck in "idea mode" that you cannot seem to bring to launch? Why?

____

____

What outdated system or decision-making processes is keeping it stuck?

____

____

What one small, imperfect action can your team take today to spark inertia?

____

____

How does the action you have chosen challenge established patterns while building toward systematic transformation?

____

____

Do your team's activities currently align with your overall mission? Why or why not?

____

____

Which activities feel productive but maintain outdated approaches rather than creating transformation?

____

____

What meetings, processes, or bottlenecks need to be removed to spark action?

____

____

What alternatives do you seek to implement to ensure your changes will stick rather than reverting to old patterns?

____

____

Where might you need to revisit your **[S]**trategy or **[P]**lanning to regain clarity?

____

____

What additional support might you need to help you determine the best next step to take?

____

____

*At Brown Transformations Consulting, we can help accelerate your transition and would love to collaborate with you. Scan the QR at the end of this chapter and take our free **S.P.A.R.K. Framework Assessment™** to identify where your team is stalled and receive customized next steps for moving forward by leveraging your results.*

For Leaders:

Moving Past Fear Into Empowered Decisions

Have you delayed action due to fear or uncertainty?

____

____

What outdated beliefs about leadership, risk, or change might be creating this hesitation?

____

____

What would aligned, courageous leadership look like in that situation?

____

____

How would this courageous action challenge established norms while building sustainable alternatives?

____

____

What single bold conversation or decision do you need to make this week?

____

____

How will this conversation model the kind of transparency and authenticity you want to see throughout your organization?

____

____

How can you model imperfect yet strategic action to your team?

____

____

How can you demonstrate that courage by taking action outside your comfort zones, demonstrating that growth matters more to you than risk?

____

____

What systems will help you to track your own leadership impact?

____

____

*At Brown Transformations Consulting, we can help accelerate your transition and would love to collaborate with you. Scan the QR at the end of this chapter and take our free **S.P.A.R.K. Framework Assessment™** to identify where your team is stalled and receive customized next steps for moving forward by leveraging your results.*

For Coaches and Consultants:

Turning Clarity Into Consistency

What one service or program have you delayed launching?

____

____

What outdated beliefs about readiness, perfection, or market conditions have created this delay?

____

____

What small action can you take that would make this offer visible to your audience today?

____

____

How does this action step challenge conventional wisdom about business development while still building authentic authority?

____

____

Where are you stuck in planning or avoiding visibility?

____

____

Which comfortable planning activities are you using that are sophisticated procrastination disguised as productivity?

____

How are you measuring the alignment of your daily tasks to your larger goals?

____

____

How could accountability help you to maintain this alignment rather than reverting to scattered activity?

____

____

What does consistent action look like for you in the next seven days?

____

____

At Brown Transformations Consulting, we can help accelerate your transition and would love to collaborate with you. Scan the QR at the end of this chapter and take our free **S.P.A.R.K. Framework Assessment™** to identify where your team is stalled and receive customized next steps for moving forward by leveraging your results.

For Individuals:

Creating Forward Motion With Intention

Where do you feel stuck or unsure about what to do next?

What outdated approaches to personal development or career growth might be creating this feeling?

What one action can you take today—even if it's uncomfortable?

How does this action challenge familiar patterns while building the life and career you actually want?

How will you track your personal progress and celebrate small wins?

How will you ensure this tracking measures both external achievements and internal transformation?

Which beliefs are inherited limitations rather than current realities, and how can you take action to test new possibilities?

What does purposeful movement look like for you this month?

How could expert guidance help you accelerate this movement and ensure it leads to systematic transformation rather than temporary change?

---

*At Brown Transformations Consulting, we can help accelerate your transition and would love to collaborate with you. Scan the QR at the end of this chapter and take our free **S.P.A.R.K. Framework Assessment*™* to identify where your team is stalled and receive customized next steps for moving forward by leveraging your results.*

You've aligned your vision, mapped your plan, and are ready to take bold, intentional action. You are ready to step outside of your comfort zone and challenge outdated approaches while building sustainable alternatives.

Just remember: **Action without measurement and continual refinement is just trial and error.**

This is why the most successful transformations happen with expert guidance. Just know that you deserve the right support to ensure lasting transformation rather than temporary change. The leaders and organizations who are redefining their industries aren't doing it alone, they're working with experts who can see blind spots, provide accountability, and accelerate the transition. They're investing in guidance that transforms the unknown into clear direction and individual effort into systematic transformation.

Quote to Close the Chapter:

Transformation doesn't wait for perfect conditions—it answers the call of aligned action. Start before you're ready and lead before it's easy.

— Dr. Michelle Brown

SCAN TO TAKE The S.P.A.R.K. Framework **Assessment™**

Next Up: Chapter 7 – [R]esults: Measure What Matters, Lead What Lasts

You've aligned your vision, mapped your plan, and taken bold, imperfect, transformational **[A]**ction. You've started challenging outdated internal systems and choosing moves that actually match the future you want to build personally and professionally. Now it's time to make sure all that movement actually *means* something.

In the next chapter, we'll shift into **[R]**esults—where you stop guessing, start measuring what truly matters, and turn your actions into visible, sustainable proof that your internal systems, culture, and leadership are really changing, not just staying busy in better-looking ways. This is where you learn to track transformation, not just activity; impact, not just effort; and progress that lasts, not just quick wins that fade.

We'll explore what most leaders and organizations get wrong about results, what to measure instead in this redefined era of leadership, and how to read your patterns as data—personally and professionally. Chapter 7 is where your **[S]**trategy, **[P]**lanning, and **[A]**ction stop living as concepts and start showing up as evidence you can point to, build on, and celebrate.

CHAPTER 7 – [R]ESULTS
MEASURE WHAT MATTERS, LEAD WHAT LATS

By now, you've set a clear strategy, mapped out a plan, and started taking **[A]**ction. You've done the internal and external work to move with intention. Now, it's time to measure the impact of your effort, but here is the warning: Transformation efforts tend to fail when they measure the wrong things, track outdated metrics, or celebrate progress using frameworks which are designed for a world that no longer exists.

Progress without reflection can lead to stale motion. The same goes for measurement without systematic transformation. We need more than sophisticated record-keeping that documents activity while missing actual breakthroughs towards human understanding.

Over time, this life of motion without meaning becomes the very definition of insanity. Repeating the same actions and expecting different outcomes is insane. Have you ever been there? In business, insanity looks like endless meetings, misaligned strategies, and exhausted teams chasing results they never see or feel.

We might admit, "This isn't working." Yet we tend to respond with the same moves:

- We add another meeting.
- We create another memo.
- We host another training.
- We launch another "initiative" stacked on top of the last one that failed.

The language changes and the slide decks are updated, but the internal systems stay exactly the same. Therefore, the outcomes do, too.

To see if you have ever been caught in a loop of insanity, let's unpack common ways that leaders unknowingly create chaos. Then, let's see what it looks like to shift from band-aid fixes to transformational action.

Insanity Pattern: What They Say → What They Do	**How This Impacts The Team**	**S.P.A.R.K.-Aligned Alternative (What to Do Instead)**	**How To Recognize It's Time For Transformational Change**
"Communication is broken." → Send more emails. Add more meetings. Record another town hall.	The team feels information overload but has no real clarity. People still don't know who decides what, where to go for answers, or what truly matters. Confusion gets louder, not better.	Use **[S]**trategy + **[P]**lanning to redesign your communication system, not just your messages. Clarify decision rights. Standardize a few key channels and use tools/AI to summarize and surface what matters. This allows people to act on it with clarity.	The same "communication issues" resurface every quarter, despite more messaging. People say, *"I don't know what's going on"* or *"No one tells us anything,"* even after a "big push." That's your sign: It's a system issue, not a messaging issue.
"People are burned out." → Offer pizza, wellness webinars, or one mental health day. Change nothing else.	The team shows short bursts of gratitude, followed by a return to overload, unrealistic timelines, and unspoken expectations. Burnout deepens because token gestures highlight how little has actually changed.	Use **[P]**lanning + **[A]**ction to rebuild how work is structured. Audit workloads. Reset priorities. Adjust staffing. Set real boundaries. Train leaders to model healthy behavior. Support with tools that remove low-value admin work.	Top performers leave, sick days rise. So does quiet quitting. The same: "We're drowning" feedback shows up on surveys. That's your signal: It's time to change how work is designed, not just how it's "celebrated."
"Engagement is low." → Run another survey. Start a committee. Host a one-off "culture day."	The team is feeling survey fatigue. People share honest feedback but see no meaningful follow-through. Cynicism grows. Engagement dips further because speaking up seems pointless.	Use **[R]**esults + **[K]**PI Knowledge to tie engagement to real decisions. Adjust manager expectations, meeting rhythms, recognition, and growth paths. Show people, *"Here's what we changed because of what you told us."*	Engagement scores dip in the same departments, with the same comments, year after year. When you hear, *"Nothing changes here,"* it's time to stop surveying for data you are not committed to acting on.

Insanity Pattern: What They Say → What They Do	How This Impacts The Team	S.P.A.R.K.-Aligned Alternative (What to Do Instead)	How To Recognize It's Time For Transformational Change
"We care about inclusion." → Schedule a single DEI training.	People from marginalized groups feel unheard, unsafe, or tokenized. Trust erodes. Leaders feel "complete" because the training happened, but the experience of work hasn't changed.	Use [S]trategy + [A]ction to embed inclusion into internal systems, including hiring, promotion, pay, decision-making, feedback, and accountability. Use data + lived experience to drive specific, tangible shifts.	Harmful patterns keep repeating. The same groups stay underrepresented in leadership. Exit interviews and informal conversations name culture as the reason people leave. That's your sign: It's time to transform internal systems, not just schedule sessions.
"We need to innovate." → Launch a hackathon. Put up idea boards and then bury most of the ideas.	People get excited briefly, then discouraged when nothing meaningful happens. Innovation becomes theater instead of practice.	Use [P]lanning and [A]ction to build repeatable pathways for ideas. This includes how they're submitted, evaluated, piloted, and funded. Use AI and internal systems to sort ideas but ensure that humans decide what aligns with strategy and values.	You keep asking for ideas, but people stop contributing or say, *"What's the point?"* That's your clue. You don't need more ideas; you need an internal system that respects and acts on ones which were shared.

You can only run these "loops" so many times before it becomes exhausting, for both you and your team. The exhaustion you feel is not a sign you're weak. It's a sign that your internal systems are outdated and ready to be restructured and streamlined.

Upon realizing this, you have a choice:

- You can keep applying band-aid fixes and name it "action."
- You can make a bold decision and say, *"We're not going to spin this same wheel again this time. We're going to change the internal system that keeps creating this experience."*

That decision is where real transformation is sparked.

When it comes to tracking change, you might wonder: "How Do I Track and Test Without Getting Overwhelmed?" It is a fair question, and I am here to offer relief. Tracking is meant to be simple and support your goals, instead of being one more operational "thing" in the way.

Real transformation is tracked, tested, and celebrated, regardless of how big or small the milestones may seem. It does not, however, mean you need 15 dashboards and a data science team to accomplish it.

Tracking within the **S.P.A.R.K. Framework Assessment™** and Ecosystem means you:

- Slow down to get clear on the shift you're trying to make.
- Decide what to monitor, which tells you if the action you took is working or not.
- Check in regularly enough to adjust, not judge.
- Pivot when needed.

Here is how:

	<u>This Means</u>	<u>Examples (Personally & Professionally)</u>
1. Define the shift	Name the specific change you're trying to see, in behavior, experience, or results.	**Personally**: "I want to stop saying yes to everything and protect my time." **Professionally**: "We want fewer last-minute fire drills and more predictable project flow."
2. Choose 2–3 things to measure	Combine numbers (*what you can count*) and stories (*what people feel and remember*).	**Personally**: Number of evenings you work late or energy level at the end of the week on a 1–10 scale. **Professionally**: Number of after-hours emergencies per month or pulse-check comments from your team on workload and clarity.
3. Set a simple review rhythm	Schedule time to look at the data and consider what you'll ask yourself in that time.	**Personally**: Weekly check-in that asks: "What helped? What drained me? What will I change next week?" **Professionally**: Monthly review that asks: "What improved? What didn't? What system or step needs adjusting?"
4. Adjust based on what you learn	Treat data as feedback, not a verdict. Remember to tweak the system, not your worth.	**Personally**: You realize late nights spike on meeting-heavy days. Therefore, you move deep work to mornings. **Professionally**: You see bottlenecks occur at one specific approval step. Therefore, you streamline or clarify that part of the process.

	This Means	**Examples (Personally & Professionally)**
5. Celebrate real movement	Notice and name progress, even when it's small. This builds momentum and trust.	**Personally**: You honor that you've kept one boundary for 3 weeks straight. **Professionally**: You share with the team, "We cut last-minute emergencies by 30% here's how, and here's what we're trying next."

Tracking what matters, both personally and professionally, is the cornerstone of sustainable growth you can see and your teams can feel.

It's the difference between:

- Leaders who document their exhaustion.
- And leaders who transform their reality, one intentional shift at a time.

This is exactly why successful leaders and organizations work with system transformation consulting firms like ours. They recognize that designing measurement systems is hard work. We love to help leaders move beyond just documenting activity, and how to create deep rooted and repeatable change, internally, which translates externally to their consumers.

I firmly believe: You can't improve what you don't measure, but measuring must go beyond creating statistics and churning numbers that look good on the surface but yield no real transformation or results. There is no point in using inherited metrics that worked for someone else's goals and during a completely different era.

Instead, we must be able to include systematic indicators of transformation—evidence that outdated internal systems are being replaced with sustainable alternatives that show how individual growth is creating organizational change, and that technological efficiency is enhancing team productivity and project execution, rather than replacing human-centered approaches.

When we track this kind of change, we have something to celebrate. Success—big or small—deserves recognition. You deserve recognition. Your team deserves recognition. When you make it easy to see what is worth celebrating, it is important to use measurement approaches that capture the depth and scope of change that you're implementing.

To begin, we must know what to measure. This helps us go beyond a category, label, or generic "one-size-fits-all" numbering systems and metrics tracking. We are seeking to track transformation, not just performance, requirements, or expectations forged from natural human biases. The goal is to see progress, intentional alignment and impact, not just productivity.

As always, these goals take us back to strategic internal changes.

As a former student-athlete, career-driven leader, and mother who navigated a balance between school, career, and life, I've always known the importance of maintaining harmony between my personal and professional life. It's at the heart of my **[S]**trategy. More than balance, however, strategy is about integration. I get to be fully whole in each role I take on. Therefore, I get to measure success in ways that honor my personal authenticity and professional excellence, while keeping individual growth and collective impact as values I get to embody daily.

For me, balance isn't about doing it all perfectly; it's about consistent progress over time and real habit changes.

In tracking my goals, I seek to support sustainable transformation rather than pursue unsustainable perfectionism. It's about being intentional and pivoting when needed. It is a joy to create internal systems that support both personal purpose and your peace.

But you might wonder, "What does this look like?"

Here is how it played out for me:

I started out as a career-driven woman, newly married, and a first-time homeowner. Before I knew it, I was expecting my first child. Life was full and changing fast, yet I still wanted a thriving career and to pursue the highest level of education while also seeking my desired leadership endeavors. However, I knew I couldn't "hope it all worked out." I needed **[S]**trategy.

I paused and took inventory of my life as it was, not as I thought it "should" be. I refused to be caught in comparison. I dared to believe my journey was mine and mine alone.

I returned to the goals I set for myself years earlier and asked:

- What have I already accomplished?
- What has evolved?
- What hasn't happened yet and why?
- What is in my control right now and what is not, but I can pivot around or through?

The reality was, some milestones had been reached; others had been surpassed. Those were my wins both "small" and "big" ones:

- I had become a first-time homeowner.
- I was building a marriage and a family.
- I was excelling in my career.
- I surpassed many of my other goals.

Other goals, like graduating with my doctorate *before* purchasing a home or having a second child, however, did not happen on my original timeline. At first, when I saw goals that weren't reached "on schedule," I felt discouraged. I told myself: *"You failed. You didn't do this in the right order."*

But here's where **[S]**trategy and self-grace met.

When I zoomed out, the truth was this: I hadn't failed. I had been winning in other areas of my life, deeply, consistently, and with intention. The evidence was all around me. I had a stable home, a loving and thriving marriage, a growing family, and a thriving career. Those were not side notes; they were part of the vision. They were proof that my life was still aligned with my larger purpose and desired end goals, even if the sequence was different than I planned.

Instead of using my missed timeline as a weapon or view it as "failure," I used it as information and an opportunity. I gave myself grace, I updated my expectations, and I created a new list of desired end goals that matched the reality of who I was becoming and not who I thought I "had" to be.

That's **[S]**trategy in real life. It tells the hard truth about where you are and redefines where you're going.

That took me to my next step: **[P]**lanning.

I knew life would not stop nor politely step aside for my personal or professional goals. There would be diapers, deadlines, long nights, leadership strains, team demands, family obligations and moments where motivation dipped. Therefore, I built a plan that honored both my ambition and my daily life.

I got clear on my desired end goal: *I will complete my doctorate program with honors by the end of December.*

At this point, I was pregnant with our second child, worked full-time at a consulting firm, went to school full-time, and supported my husband in his career as a head football coach. That meant my **[P]**lanning couldn't be theoretical, it had to be actionable and realistic.

To put my plan in motion, I:

- Communicated clearly with my husband about my goals. Together, we defined how we could support each other in this season.
- Created a robust academic schedule that matched my real capacity, not my fantasy energy.
- Designed my days in alignment with what mattered most, including my coursework, family, faith, health, and work commitments.

Then came **[A]**ction—which looked like:

- Choosing to write the paper, even when I was exhausted.
- Remaining disciplined to still take action when it didn't feel like anything was working in my favor or according to plan.
- Waking up early or staying up a little later to study when the house was finally quiet.
- Saying **no** to distractions that did not align with my end goals, even when they were good things.
- Honoring the professional and personal academic schedule I set—one meeting, one class, one assignment, and one discussion post at a time.

My **incremental wins** looked like:

- Sticking to the academic schedule I created, even on the hard days.
- Caring for my family, while pregnant with my second child, even when exhausted.
- Completing my professional tasks early or on time.
- Leading our sales team and client projects with excellence, even in times of unforeseen chaos and last minute requests.

Those weren't just "nice moments." Those were my **[R]**esults.

[R]esults in that season were not only about a diploma with honors at the end (*although that mattered*). **[R]**esults were also the small things that were maintained:

- A stronger marriage because we communicated and planned together.
- A more grounded sense of identity as a mother, sibling, wife *and* a professional.
- A track record of follow-through where others trusted in me.
- Evidence that my internal systems, routines, boundaries, and commitments were working.

And finally, I built my **[K]**PI Knowledge—my own internal dashboard of what worked, what didn't, and what I wanted to carry forward into the next season.

[K]PI Knowledge I learned included:

- "When I batch my schoolwork and career tasks on specific days and times, I feel less scattered."
- "When I communicate my deadlines and needs ahead of time, my home and work life flow better."
- "When I ignore my capacity and try to be superwoman, everything suffers—including me."

Those learnings became my measured and tracked data about my life and my career. They informed me how I choose future goals, how I structured my time, and how I led teams. Eventually, they became pillars that defined how I built Brown Transformations Consulting and client success stories. They led me to form my personal **S.P.A.R.K. Framework Playbook™**.

Everything I learned is available to you too. Every small step counts as evidence.

Your timeline may not look the way you imagined. Some goals may take longer. Some may have arrived early. Others may still be in progress or foggy. That doesn't mean you're behind, it might simply mean you're building something more holistic, grounded, and aligned than you originally planned.

You can bring your own life through the **S.P.A.R.K. Framework Assessment™** the same way:

- Revisit your **[S]**trategy: What season are you really in and what truly matters now?
- Refine your **[P]**lanning: What path fits your reality, not your expectations of perfectionism?
- Commit to **[A]**ction: What is one aligned step you can take this week?
- Notice your **[R]**esults: Where are you already winning more than you give yourself credit for?
- Capture your **[K]**PI Knowledge: What are you learning about yourself that you want to continue to carry forward?

Just in case you feel caught in a comparison loop, or are concerned that you have not met your goals within the timeframe you had for yourself or your deadline, first become aware of it, then pivot as needed, and finally consider one way to shift the mindset:

<u>Comparison Traps Sound Like…</u>	**<u>A Holistic Perspective Sounds Like …</u>**
"I should be at *this* title/level by *this* age."	"My path is seasonal and unique. The timing of my milestones doesn't disqualify me; it reflects the life I'm building."
"Everyone else seems further ahead, maybe I'm behind."	"I measure progress by alignment, growth, and impact, not by titles, timelines, or highlight reels."
"If my career is not linear, I must have messed up."	"Non-linear doesn't mean broken. It means I've gained range, resilience, and perspective that traditional paths often don't build."
"I can't slow down or pivot; I'll lose my place."	"Pausing, pivoting, or re-aligning is strategy, not failure. I can reset my internal systems and still rise."
"My worth is defined by how closely I match the 'ideal' career story."	"My worth is rooted in who I am and how I serve. My career is one expression of that, not the whole story."

When you stop comparing yourself to a traditional script and start honoring your own **S.P.A.R.K.**, you stop chasing someone else's timeline and start leading your own.

The funny thing about comparison is the same thing happens inside organizations. They compare themselves to traditional success metrics and inherited scorecards, even when those measures are misaligned with the impact they say they want to make. In the same way that professionals can get trapped chasing titles and timelines that don't reflect their true calling, institutions can get trapped chasing numbers that don't reflect their true purpose or connect to overall goals of each department for the business.

That's exactly what was happening in this next example.

Consider the transformation of Dr. Lisa Thompson, Chief Innovation Officer at a major academic medical center. She faced the challenge of measuring research impact in ways that honored both scientific rigor and patient outcomes. Traditional academic measurement focuses on publications, citations, and grant funding. Each of these metrics tend to incentivize research that advances careers versus advancing patient care.

Dr. Thompson decided to go against this grain. She didn't just track different numbers; she systematically transformed how her institution approached research measurement. Instead of just counting publications, they measured real-world application and patient impact. Instead of tracking funding amounts, they measured collaboration across disciplines and community engagement. Instead of documenting individual researcher achievements, they measured systematic improvements to healthcare delivery.

The results they achieved revolutionized their approach to medical research. Research teams began focusing on projects that held immediate clinical relevance. Collaboration between departments increased dramatically. Community health outcomes have improved measurably. Other academic medical centers began adopting their measurement approaches, creating industry-wide change.

To make Dr. Thompson's transformation tangible, here's her story through our Obstacle → Opportunity → Option → Outcome lens, with **[R]**esults and **[K]**PI Knowledge at the center.

Summary

Obstacle	As Chief Innovation Officer at a major academic medical center, Dr. Lisa Thompson was under pressure to "prove impact." Traditional academic metrics, publications, citations, and grant dollars—rewarded research that advanced careers more than it advanced patient care. The internal measurement system was misaligned with their true mission.
Opportunity	Instead of treating this as a "we need more research" problem, she named the real issue: It was a measurement problem. The way they defined and tracked "success" was pulling attention away from what mattered most, real-world application, patient outcomes, and community impact. That realization turned reporting into a lever for transformation.
[R] & [K] Approach – What She Did Differently	Using the **S.P.A.R.K. Framework™**, Dr. Thompson systematically transformed how the institution measured research impact. They: (1) tracked real-world application and patient outcomes, not just publication counts; (2) measured collaboration across disciplines, not just individual achievements; (3) included community engagement and health outcomes as key indicators; and (4) captured system-level improvements to care delivery. These became core **[K]**PIs baked into dashboards, reviews, promotions, and strategic decisions.
Outcome	Measurement stopped being a historical report and became a strategic tool. Research teams began choosing projects with immediate clinical relevance. Cross-department collaboration surged. Community health outcomes improved in measurable ways. Other academic medical centers started adopting their model. Dr. Thompson proved that when you transform what you measure and how you learn from it, you don't just change reports, you change behavior, culture, and impact across an entire industry.

That's the power and flexibility of the **S.P.A.R.K. Framework Assessment™**. It cuts through practices that no longer serve the culture or customers and replaces them with intentional, future-focused solutions. It creates measurement approaches that support transformation rather than documenting activity alone. It works at any level, in every phase of growth, regardless of one's background or lived experience. Why? Because it measures what matters to sustainable transformation versus what's comfortable or familiar. Dr. Thompson's story shows us that **[R]**esults and **[K]**PI Knowledge aren't about collecting more numbers; they're about choosing to focus on the *right* ones.

When it comes to **[R]**esults, let's discuss the common mistakes we tend to make and why. Traditional measurement approaches focus on HR metrics, exit interview data, satisfaction surveys, and retention statistics, but these measurements often miss the systematic issues that create the symptoms they're documenting.

They measure the problems without measuring the transformation and the positive impact from that transformation.

To take it to the organizational level, too often, companies focus solely on quarterly earnings, ROI, lead conversions, and external KPIs. While yes, these numbers matter, they're only one small piece of the larger puzzle. More problematically, traditional metrics often reinforce internal systems and approaches that actually need to be transformed. They measure efficiency within outdated frameworks rather than transformation toward sustainable alternatives.

What's often missing? Human metrics, transformation markers, and systematic change indicators that show how outdated attempts are replaced with sustainable alternatives. Human metrics that focus on "why" professionals and communities need specific things are often missing. Transformation metrics that track systematic change rather than activity are also often missing. Along with the integration of metrics that show technological efficiency, enhancing human-centered approaches, rather than replacing those approaches is often missing.

Transformation and long-term sustainability require a deeper lens. It's not enough to track what's easy to count or what looks good in a boardroom report, but let's admit: This is hard when tracking the wrong things. Why? Because it's challenging to see the whole internal system clearly when you're leading from inside of it. That's why so many leaders find themselves drowning in dashboards, reports, and KPIs, yet still asking, *"Why aren't we really changing?"*

The first thing to determine is if a measurement is rooted in ego or fear-based tactics.

- Ego-based measurement asks, *"How does this make me look?"* instead of *"What does this teach us?"* Numbers become a mirror for personal status rather than a window into truth. Leaders cling to vanity metrics that impress, but don't transform or provide real impact.
- Fear-based measurement uses metrics as weapons instead of wisdom: *"Hit this number or else."* Public rankings shame professionals, dashboards fuel anxiety, not alignment, and people start hiding mistakes, gaming numbers, and protecting themselves instead of improving themselves.

When measurement is driven by ego and fear, you don't get better results; you get performance. You get short-term spikes that sabotage long-term health. You get teams who are busy surviving the scorecard and burning out, instead of improving themselves or the internal systems.

I am daring us to be different.

There is a way forward which is rooted in holistic, purpose-driven approaches with clear communication and clarity.

It asks questions like:

- *Are we living our values as we pursue results?*
- *Are our internal systems improving, or are we just pushing people harder?*
- *Are our metrics reflecting the humans we serve—our teams and our consumers—or just the numbers we've always reported?*

We have an opportunity to shift away from metrics that protect ego and fuel fear and move toward metrics that reveal truth, honor people, and guide real transformation.

Consider a Chief Financial Officer at a major energy corporation. We'll call him Marcus Washington. He's facing a familiar challenge: measuring financial performance while the business transitions toward more sustainable energy practices.

In most energy organizations, traditional metrics still dominate: extraction efficiency, cost per barrel, and short-term profit margins. Those numbers may look impressive quarter to quarter, but they quietly resist the very innovations needed for long-term survival and relevance.

A CFO in Marcus's position can choose to do more than bolt a few sustainability metrics onto an old reporting package. Instead, they can systematically transform how financial performance is defined and measured during industry transition.

That kind of shift might look like developing integrated measurement approaches that:

- Track both current operational efficiency **and** investment in future capabilities.
- Balance immediate profitability **and** long-term market positioning, instead of pitting them against each other.
- Consider shareholder value **and** stakeholder impact, employees, communities, regulators, and the environment.

When a finance leader leads this way, the corporation can reposition itself as an industry leader in a period of massive change. Investor confidence grows because the market can see a clear, systematic approach to transition, not reactive moves. Employee retention improves as people feel proud of their company's forward-thinking leadership. Over time, the measurement model itself becomes something other energy companies start watching and learning from.

To see how this plays out, here's this kind of transformation through the lens of Obstacle → Opportunity → Option → Outcome, with **[R]**esults and **[K]**PI Knowledge at the center.

<u>**Summary**</u>

Obstacle	A CFO at a major energy corporation is responsible for financial performance during a massive industry shift toward sustainable energy. Traditional energy metrics—extraction efficiency, cost per barrel, short-term profit margins—are still driving decisions. Those measures reward the old model and quietly penalize long-term sustainability investments.
Opportunity	Instead of treating this as "we just need better returns," he names the real issue: The measurement system is anchoring them to the past. As long as success is defined only by traditional financial metrics, any move toward sustainability will *look* like a loss, even when it's actually smart, strategic evolution. That realization turns reporting into a lever for change.
[R] & [K] Approach – What He Does Differently	By applying the **S.P.A.R.K. Framework™** with **[R]**esults and **[K]**PI Knowledge at the center, he systematically transforms how financial performance is measured. They: **(1)** track both current operational efficiency and investment in future capabilities (renewables, new tech, new skills); **(2)** measure immediate profitability *and* long-term market positioning; and **(3)** include shareholder value *and* stakeholder impact (communities, regulators, employees, environment). These integrated metrics are built into **[K]**PI systems—financial reports, strategy reviews, investor communication, and internal decisions.
Outcome	Financial reporting stops glorifying only what the old model rewards. It starts spotlighting the real drivers of long-term resilience, trust, and relevance. The corporation positions itself as an industry leader during massive change. Investor confidence rises, employees feel proud of the direction, and other energy companies begin watching the model as a blueprint. This kind of shift shows that when you change what you track, you change what you dare to do. Measurement becomes a catalyst for evolution, not an anchor to outdated practices.

Marcus's story shows us something powerful: when you only measure what the old model rewards, you keep getting the old results. When you start measuring what truly drives long-term value, future capabilities, stakeholder trust, organizational culture, and alignment, you unlock a completely different kind of return on investment (ROI).

It's true for every leader and every organization who is asking: "If we say people are our greatest asset, are we actually measuring what's *happening* to our people?"

That means tracking what matters to the humans who are driving your business, such as:

- **Behavioral patterns** and **team dynamics** that show systematic culture transformation rather than surface-level policy changes.
- **Recruiting behaviors** that intentionally reflect your target audience and demonstrate a commitment to authentic diversity, not checkbox compliance.

- **Retention rates** that reveal whether people stay because of authentic alignment or because they need a paycheck.
- **Employee satisfaction**, **engagement**, and **well-being** metrics that capture individual fulfillment and collective transformation.
- **Alignment between internal culture** and **external brand perception** that demonstrates authentic change, not just a marketing rebrands.
- **Team collaboration**, **innovation output**, and **execution quality** metrics that show how work is done differently, not just how much activity is happening.

Always remember: [R]esults are more than numbers; they're stories behind the numbers. They're evidence of systematic transformation and proof that outdated approaches have been replaced with sustainable alternatives. They're indicators that individual growth is creating organizational change. Your solution to success is hidden in the patterns.

The **S.P.A.R.K. Framework™** doesn't choose between internal systems *or* organizational culture; it aligns both. How? By redesigning internal systems such as how goals are set, decisions are made, and performance is measured *and* by reshaping the organization's culture, such as how people show up, speak up, collaborate, and lead. With both areas combined, these efforts reinforce each other instead of pull in opposite directions.

This matters because:

- You can't get sustainable [R]esults if you have a great organizational culture, but broken internal systems.
- You also can't get sustainable [R]esults if you have polished internal systems, but a fear-based, burned-out organizational culture.

Real transformation happens when measurement, internal systems, and organizational cultures work together.

Through the **S.P.A.R.K. Framework™** we connect:

- **Strategy with performance.** What you say you care about is what you actually track and reward.
- **Purpose with impact.** Your "why" shows up in your "what" and "how."
- **Culture with [R]esults.** The way people treat each other and work together is directly reflected in the outcomes you measure.
- **Individual transformation with organizational change.** People aren't growing in isolation due to the internal systems they work in.
- **Technological efficiency with human-centered values.** AI and tech tools amplify your people instead of erasing them.

- **Immediate outcomes with long-term systematic transformation.** You're not just fixing today's fires; you're building tomorrow's foundation.

In other words: The **S.P.A.R.K. Framework™** doesn't just change what you track; it changes what you're tracking to make your impact possible.

Next, let's unpack how we can leverage the **[R]**esults Pillar across different roles and responsibilities. To begin, let's start with Organizations and Teams and work through a scenario.

[R]esults Pillar: For Organizations and Teams

Scenario: A company's revenue is growing, but employee turnover is high. Engagement scores are flat and leadership is baffled. They know they need to realign, but don't know where to start or how.

S.P.A.R.K. Framework™ – [R]esults Approach

Revisit [S]trategy: Prioritize people-centered values in leadership development, but don't just *say* it. Measure it through transformation indicators, versus policy announcements or training completion rates.

Ask:

- Are leaders leading differently, or did they just attend a workshop?
- Are we seeing changes in how decisions are made, how feedback is received, and how people are treated in authentic moments of tension?

To track what matters most, and not just what's easiest to pull from a dashboard, it means tracking:

- **Retention rates.** Determine who is staying, who is leaving, and why. Ask: Are we retaining the people we say we want to build our legacy with?
- **Hiring rates and practices.** Ask: Are we diversifying who we hire, where we look, and how we evaluate talent? Or are we repeating old patterns with new language?"
- **Psychological safety indicators.** Determine what signals are present which indicate whether people feel safe enough to:

  - Speak their ideas and concerns.
  - Admit mistakes without fear of punishment.
  - Disagree respectfully with leadership.
  - Ask for help before things break.
  - Tell the truth about important issues

Curious what Psychological Safety Indicators To Look For?

Consider these displays:

<u>What to Look For</u>	<u>How to Measure Psychological Safety</u>
Pulse survey questions	• "I feel safe speaking up when something isn't working." • "My leader listens when I raise a concern." • "Mistakes are treated as learning opportunities, not as weapons."
Meeting behaviors	• Who talks and who never does? • Do the same voices dominate meetings? • Do ideas only flow downward, or are they also upward and across?
Idea and feedback flow	• Do people submit ideas, raise issues, and use feedback channels? • How often does feedback from the front lines lead to visible change?
Error and incident reporting	• Do people flag risks early, or only when things are on fire? • Do people hide problems for fear of reaction?

These habits and behaviors are a reflection of whether your people believe it's safe to be honest, human, and engaged at work. Therefore, yes—track retention, hiring rates, psychological safety indicators, and team innovation output, beyond just quotas and sales goals, but don't treat them as random performance stats. Treat each signal as evidence and proof that your internal systems and leadership behaviors are or are not actually changing.

Additional sample metrics to track include:

- Employee Net Promoter Score (eNPS) that shows systematic trust-building rather than just momentary satisfaction. Cross-department collaboration scores that demonstrate systematic breakdown of silos rather than just project completion rates are also available.
- Staff-led initiative counts and implementation that show empowerment rather than "suggestion box" activity.
- Revenue growth and employee initiatives integrated to show alignment between people satisfaction and business outcomes.
- Internal DEIB alignment reports that measure culture transformation rather than compliance.

The **[R]**esult we find is that leadership begins to recognize hidden organizational culture gaps. Once **[R]**esults indicate we are moving in the right direction, the next step is to use **[K]**PI Knowledge to go deeper than numbers, which will be covered in the next chapter.

Next, let's unpack how to leverage the **[R]**esults Pillar as a leader.

[R]esults Pillar: For Leaders – Leading What Lasts

Scenario: A department head keeps hitting their target numbers, but burnout, conflict, and turnover are rising under their watch. Focusing solely on performance metrics, revenue targets, productivity, and efficiency ratios has created systematic leadership issues that have led to unsustainable short-term results. The root issues? This leader has been stuck measuring outcomes without measuring the health of the approach that has created such outcomes.

Therefore, the leader turns to the **S.P.A.R.K. Framework™**.

Here is the [R]esults Approach:

- **Reassess [P]lanning**

  Revisit how planning happens. Determine what is leading the work, goals, and expectations. Balance productivity with sustainability. Don't just "lighten the load" on paper. Measure whether planning changes how work feels and functions.

  Ask: Are deadlines more realistic? Are last-minute fire drills decreasing? Is the workload more equitable across the team?

- **Use [A]ction to co-create new team norms**

  Co-create new norms around communication, boundaries, responsiveness, and support. Then, measure the implementation and consistency, not just the announcement.

  Ask: Are these "norms" visible in meetings, emails, and decision-making? Are leaders modeling them, or simply asking others to follow them?

- **Track emotional intelligence, feedback cycles, and well-being. Do this systematically, not randomly.**

  Build rhythms, such as regular upward feedback, consistent 1:1s, pulse surveys, and honest check-ins, that determine whether people feel safe, heard, and supported over time. These aren't "soft extras." They are hard, leading indicators of whether your leadership approach is sustainable or quietly burning people out—all while numbers look good on paper.

Sample metrics to track include:

- Managerial trust ratings that show deep relationship-building versus momentary approval.
- Burnout indicators during staff check-ins. These demonstrate systematic prevention rather than just crisis intervention.
- Psychological safety assessments that measure culture transformation versus survey responses.
- Feedback implementation rate that indicates responsiveness versus idea collection.

[R]esult: By tracking properly, the leader shifts from reactive management to reflective leadership. They drive results with their people, not at the expense of them. More importantly, they create a leadership model that other managers take note of and begin to replicate, proving that systematic transformation creates competitive advantage.

To find out how to leverage the **[R]esults** Pillar as a coach and consultant, let's dive into another scenario.

[R]esults Pillar: For Coaches and Consultants – [R]esults That Build Authority

Scenario: A consultant is booking clients but has not secured repeat contracts or referrals.

Traditional measurement approaches would focus on business metrics, including revenue per client, contract length, and referral rates. But these measurements often miss the deeper issue, the client nurturing process. Without this, the consultant will struggle to form recurring, long-term client relationships. Measuring transactions without measuring transformation and retention means there is opportunity left untapped. To take it a step further, this consultant is not asking the right question. The deeper question at hand is, "Why are my clients leaving or not returning?"

Using the **S.P.A.R.K. Framework™,** the first step is to use **[S]**trategy to clarify brand promise and transformation outcomes. To do so, measure via client transformation indicators versus tracking your marketing message consistency.

- Implement feedback tools and values-aligned deliverables but measure the impact these create for client success instead of just client satisfaction of the process.
- Use **[R]**esults to refine services and articulate client impact. To do so, measure transformation found within the client's organization as opposed to tracking client achievement alone.

The goal is to do more than just improve client satisfaction. Consulting is a gift. It holds the opportunity to transform your entire approach to service delivery. There is nothing more satisfying as a coach or consultant than to be able to support others by them achieving consistent transformation results. When reaching this level of impact, it will generate organic referrals, build long-term relationships, and have you collaborating once more with returning clients.

Sample metrics to track include:

- **Client satisfaction scores.** This indicates value in the delivery rather than ranking service ratings alone.
- **Referral request frequency.** This demonstrates trust-building has occurred rather than networking effectiveness.
- **Client transformation testimonials.** These document systematic change rather than state positive experience.
- **Retention or recurring contract rates.** that show systematic ongoing value creation rather than just initial project success.

[R]esult: The consultant leverages data to strengthen their service positioning, increase client satisfaction, and expand their authority.

Let's dive into how to leverage the **[R]**esults Pillar as an individual.

[R]esults Pillar: For Individuals – Tracking Progress with Purpose

Scenario: An individual is busy but feels like they're never "doing enough." They can't see their progress. They only feel the overwhelm.

Traditional metrics focus on productivity, goals completed, habits maintained, and achievements unlocked. But these measurements often miss building deep personal transformation from within that creates lasting fulfillment. Instead, they only measure activity without checking for authentic alignment or sustainable progress.

S.P.A.R.K. Framework™ – [R]esults Approach:

- Revisit **[S]**trategy to calibrate towards qualitative growth, not just output. Celebrate the internal milestones you have already achieved personally and professionally. Measure the alignment you have, or lack thereof, between your personal values and professional choices versus focusing solely on external achievement.
- Create a personal dashboard of intentional habits and milestones, reflect regularly, and revise as needed. Measure transformation in terms of your personal growth rather than just tracking completion rates.

We want to support you and help you identify these metrics. You can begin by scanning the QR code at the end of this chapter. Our goal is for you to go beyond simply tracking better metrics. We want you to systematically transform your entire approach to personal and professional development, creating sustainable growth that impacts every area of your life.

Looking for a few metrics to start with? Consider these.

Sample metrics to track:

1. **Weekly habit streaks** (i.e. movement, reflection, induced levels of anxiety, etc.) that reveal self-awareness has increased versus just behavioral compliance.
2. **Emotional resilience** during stressful moments (i.e. avoiding paralysis) demonstrates systematic transformation in how you navigate challenges rather than just stress management.
3. **Time spent on passion projects** or **aligned goals** (i.e. movement towards a goal, not motion or busyness) shows an integration of authentic purpose versus just productivity optimization.
4. **Wins journal** or **self-recognition lists** which document personal transformation versus achievement tracking alone.

[R]esult: Putting these metrics in place provides several positive results. For one, self-awareness increases. Confidence builds. You think in terms of progress, not just productivity. With your development in sight, you become even more invigorated to progress further. More importantly, you develop systematic approaches to growth that create sustainable transformation instead of being trapped in cyclical improvement efforts.

Whether you're an individual seeking personal and professional alignment, a leader navigating organizational transformation, or an organization that is redefining industry standards, you have what it takes to measure what matters and track the transformation that provides lasting results.

The leaders and organizations who are redefining their industries aren't just working harder or trying more strategies; they're restructuring how they have been measuring their efforts. They ensure that any measurement they track supports the changes they're seeking from within rather than reinforcing the limitations they're trying to overcome.

Quote to Close the Chapter:

If you're not measuring what matters, you're managing what's comfortable. Documenting activity isn't transformation—breakthrough comes when leaders measure what others miss.

— Dr. Michelle Brown

SCAN TO TAKE The S.P.A.R.K. Framework **Assessment™**

Next Up: Chapter 8 – [K]PI Knowledge: Reflect, Refine, Re-Ignite

Now that you've learned how to measure what truly matters in Chapter 7—how to move beyond vanity metrics, read the story behind your numbers, and track transformation instead of just activity—you're no longer guessing about your growth. You've seen how **[R]**esults can reveal patterns in your internal systems, spotlight what's working, and expose what's quietly holding you back. You've started to see your data as proof, not just reports—as evidence of who you're becoming as a leader, a team, an organization, and a whole human.

Next, in Chapter 8, you'll learn what to *do* with all of that. Chapter 8 is where **[K]**PI Knowledge comes to life—where numbers, stories, and lived experience turn into wisdom, decisions, and upgraded internal systems. You'll learn how to pause before rushing to the next goal, reflect through a holistic lens, and refine your **S.P.A.R.K.** based on what your results are actually telling you. Instead of reacting from **F.E.A.R.** or inherited frameworks, you'll practice using informed insight to revise, realign, and re-ignite your next moves.

By the end of Chapter 8, you'll know how to: turn your results into clear lessons instead of self-judgment, spot where you're still running outdated leadership patterns, identify where your greatest transformation is already unfolding, and choose your next aligned step with confidence. You'll leave with reflection tools, tables, and questions you can revisit again and again—so **[K]**PI Knowledge becomes your ongoing engine for continuous transformation, not a one-time exercise.

CHAPTER 8 – [K]PI KNOWLEDGE
REFLECT, REFINE, RE-IGNITE

Now that you have set a clear strategy, mapped out a plan, taken intentional action, and tracked real results, transformation doesn't end there. Now we gather knowledge from what we have learned. After this, it must continue to evolve, especially if it has been a while since the learnings have been revisited. But here's what most people miss: The [K]PI Knowledge gathering process must be done correctly. If it is contaminated by outdated mindsets or internal systems that refuse to transform—then there are no new learnings, therefore, no new outcomes.

The traditional approach to "lessons learned" allows flawed assumptions regarding objectivity, neutrality, and universal best practices to remain. When inherent bias is embedded in legacy systems, they're designed to validate existing approaches rather than accept the growth which has come from challenging them. In short: They confirm what is comfortable, rather than expose what needs to be changed.

Chapter 8 is where we slow down to speed up. In this section, wisdom becomes your compass. Self-awareness becomes your strategy. Pausing to examine and replace stale patterns breaks the cycle of attempted improvement rather than discovering breakthrough transformation.

[K]PI Knowledge goes beyond stating what worked. It records *why* it worked or didn't work. From there, it helps us to understand how to continue to improve and sustain growth over time, even when circumstances shift around us. With [K]PI Knowledge we get to examine whether what "worked" actually moved you toward the desired outcome or just created a better performance mode. Through this last stage in the **S.P.A.R.K. Framework™**, we get to question whether our definition of "success" reflects authentic progress or simply mimics inherited assumptions about "what matters".

Insights gathered correctly lead us to intentional evolution. We develop systematic intelligence rather than just documenting experience. This allows us to continuously discard outdated approaches while building sustainable alternatives that can adapt to any future circumstance.

Let's take a look at Dr. Rachel Kim, Dean of Engineering at a major research university. She discovered that their traditional academic assessment methods were systematically favoring a narrow group of students. The system rewarded those who could memorize, test well, and conform to conventional academic norms, while overlooking students whose innovative thinking, creative problem-solving, and real-world application skills didn't fit standard evaluation patterns. Dr. Kim knew this wasn't a "student performance" problem; it was an internal systems problem. The way they measured success was misaligned with the kind of engineers they claimed to develop. So instead of tweaking grading criteria at the edges, she led a complete reset of how the college approached knowledge assessment and student evaluation.

Rather than measuring compliance with established academic conventions, they began assessing innovative thinking, collaborative problem-solving, and real-world application abilities. Instead of ranking students purely against inherited academic standards, they measured individual learning styles, growth, and each student's unique contribution. The results were transformative. Student engagement rose sharply as learners felt seen and valued for authentic contributions instead of just exam performance. Cross-disciplinary collaboration and community-based projects expanded. Industry partnerships grew as employers recognized graduates who could think systematically, work across disciplines, and solve real problems. Other engineering programs began adopting their assessment approaches—proving that challenging inherited evaluation methods doesn't just change grades, it changes culture and the future of the field.

It becomes reactive, not responsive; you're operating in motion, not movement.

To see what it looks like when a leader refuses that breakdown and uses the **S.P.A.R.K. Framework™** to redesign their internal systems, consider the transformation of Dr. Rachel Kim.

Summary

Obstacle

As Dean of Engineering, Dr. Kim realized their traditional assessments were rewarding memorization, test-taking, and conformity to academic norms—while overlooking students with innovative thinking, creative problem-solving, and real-world application skills. The system favored compliance over true capability.

Opportunity

She recognized a growing gap between the program's stated mission ("develop real-world problem solvers") and the metrics that actually drove decisions (GPAs, standardized exams, citation-style achievements). This wasn't a student problem; it was a measurement and internal systems problem.

[R] & [K] Approach – What She Did Differently

Using a **S.P.A.R.K.**-aligned lens, Dr. Kim led a focused reset: (1) redefining what "success" meant for their engineers; (2) piloting new assessments that evaluated innovative thinking, collaboration, and real-world application; and (3) using **[R]**esults and **[K]**PI Knowledge to refine and scale the new model across key courses and programs. Measurement stopped asking, "Who fits the old mold?" and started asking, "Who is growing into a true engineer?"

Outcome

Assessments and internal systems became aligned with the future of engineering: innovation, collaboration, and impact. Student engagement climbed, industry partnerships expanded, and other engineering programs began adopting their model. Dr. Kim showed that, when you transform what you measure and how you learn from it, you don't just change scores—you change culture, opportunity, and the future of the field.

When leaders do the opposite of what Dr. Kim did and they measure outcomes from fear-based and outdated leadership frameworks, results become reactive, not responsive. This leads us to operate in motion, not movement. It becomes an exercise in simply collecting information, versus developing intelligence.

Information only reflects raw data. It simply summarizes reports, dashboards, surveys, and endless decks.

Intelligence goes far beyond this. It's what happens when you pause, interpret that data through your [S]trategy and values, and let the information shape what you change, what you stop, and what you build next. Such habits lead us only to document experience, versus take the opportunity to create informed internal systems from systematic wisdom. Experience must be more than simply "what happened." Systematic wisdom allows you to turn that experience into new decision rules, clearer guardrails, refined internal systems, and leadership practices that make the next decision better than the last.

This gap is especially dangerous for leaders who mistake an analysis of inherited data for an objective assessment of transformation potential. Whether due to political instability, internal shifts, leadership turnover, or global crises, companies often panic. This results in scrambling to appear proactive by throwing resources at fleeting problems. In the process, it is easy to abandon long-term strategy for Band-Aid fixes, often at the expense of ROI (return on investment), trust, and organizational culture. More than that, leaders slide back into distorted decision-making frameworks that prioritize familiar solutions over systematic transformation.

But what if there was another way?

Take the story of James Mitchell, Chief Strategy Officer at a major financial services firm. James realized that his company's market analysis and competitive intelligence systems had systematically filtered information to confirm existing business model assumptions rather than expose what opportunities existed that could transform and challenge industry conventions. James didn't just gather different data; he transformed *how* the organization approached market intelligence. He dared to be different. Instead of analyzing competitors to beat them within existing frameworks, his team began studying transformation patterns across industries to identify new innovation opportunities. Instead of measuring market share within traditional banking categories, they started measuring value creation potential across emerging financial service models.

They dared to look forward instead of simply repeating past approaches and patterns.

This shift repositioned their firm from industry follower to industry innovator. They identified and capitalized on opportunities competitors missed because of inherited assumptions. Employee engagement rose as teams felt empowered to think beyond "how banking has always been done." Most importantly, their strategic intelligence model became the standard other firms began studying and implementing. This is where [K] in the **S.P.A.R.K. Framework™—[K]**PI Knowledge—comes into play. James' team proves that knowledge is more than reflection. It is an engine for refinement, re-alignment, and re-structure. **[K]**PI Knowledge, when designed well, doesn't exist to validate familiar approaches. It exists to challenge inherited assumptions and expose transformation opportunities.

By following this approach, you get a chance to pause, assess, and realign *without* discarding the progress you've already made.

[K]PI Knowledge is the pivot point. It's the key to distinguish between progress that reinforces old limitations and progress that creates transformation you can see and feel. It's the moment where, instead of starting over, you move forward *smarter*. Within this definition, you get to develop your own authentic intelligence that supports continuous transformation. That's the power of the **S.P.A.R.K. Framework™**—it doesn't break when things change. It flexes with you, helping you adapt while staying grounded. It gives you internal systems that support transformation, instead of slightly better performance inside limiting structures.

Such systematic intelligence development reveals opportunities for transformation, instead of just recording what already isn't working. It challenges inherited assumptions instead of endlessly analyzing them. Therefore, it turns information into informed internal systems of wisdom, not just more rhetoric and noise that feels like movement.

You might wonder, "How can I use this level of **[K]**PI Knowledge to benefit myself and my world?" To that, I would say it is an intensely unique process for each leader, family, and organization. After all, data isn't just for dashboards, it is gathered from each of our lived experiences, our patterns, our decisions, and the internal systems we individually keep returning to. Therefore, we must determine our own **[K]**PI Knowledge by taking the time to slow down long enough to ask: *What have I learned which is based on inherited, outdated defaults?*

To help unpack that question, I want to offer an exercise which will guide you through four different angles which dive into our unique lens. Keep in mind, not all questions will apply. In fact, many will overlap and that's the point. You are, after all, the same human inside and outside of your workplace.

Use what lands. Skip what doesn't. This is your space to be honest, not perfect.

For the next few pages, you have a chance to reflect through four lenses:

- **Organizations & Teams**: How your group, department, or company is evolving.
- **Leaders**: How you show up in positions of influence, whether formal or informal.
- **Coaches & Consultants**: How you guide, serve, and create transformation for others.
- **Individuals**: How you design your life beyond cultural programming and expectations.

You don't have to answer every question right now. Circle the ones that tug at you. Come back to the rest later. This is about awareness, not performance or perfection.

For Organizations & Teams

Strategic Growth from the Inside Out – Beyond Industry Conventions

Question	Notes
What internal behaviors or processes are helping us grow?	
Which internal behaviors or processes are holding us back?	
How are we currently tracking team cohesion, collaboration, and morale—not just output?	
Do our collaboration measures capture real transformation regarding how people work together, or are we monitoring activity and attendance alone?	
Where are we siloed or disconnected across departments or leadership levels?	
Which of these silos might be symptoms of inherited organizational structures that need transformation beyond better communication alone?	
Are our strategic goals clearly understood at every level of the organization?	
Do our strategic goals represent real transformation opportunities, or are they simply more sophisticated versions of industry-standard objectives?	

Question	**Notes**
What legacy are we building as a team or organization?	
How does our current culture support—or work against—that legacy?	

For Leaders

From Pressure to Purposeful Leadership – Beyond Conventional Wisdom

Question	**Notes**
What leadership habits have I developed that best serve my team and vision?	
Which of my "effective" leadership habits might be sourced from inherited patterns that limit transformation?	
Right now, am I leading more from pressure or from purpose?	
Is my sense of purpose authentically mine, or shaped by inherited ideas of what a "good leader" should be?	
What recent leadership decision am I most proud of—and why?	
Did that decision reflect real transformation in how I lead, or just better execution of the same old model?	
Where have I leaned into growth, even when it was uncomfortable?	

Question   **Notes**

Was that discomfort rooted in breaking old patterns or from pushing myself harder inside familiar ones?

How am I modeling alignment between my personal values and our organizational goals?

Do my stated values reflect who I truly am, or who I think I'm supposed to be as a leader?

For Coaches & Consultants

Refining Your Impact – Beyond Industry Standards

Question   **Notes**

What client transformations am I most proud of—and what made them possible?

Do these transformations reflect real change in how my clients operate, or just better performance inside the same limitations?

Am I building a sustainable business model—or quietly burning out while serving others?

Is my idea of "sustainable" based on my true capacity and values, or on inherited industry expectations?

What part of my own **S.P.A.R.K.** journey needs reflection or recalibration right now?

Is that recalibration driven by genuine transformation opportunities, or by pressure to match industry norms?

Question   **Notes**

Are my current offers aligned with my personal long-term vision plus my clients' actual needs?

Does my long-term vision reflect a new way of creating value, or is it a polished version of standard consulting models?

What feedback am I avoiding—and why?

Could that avoided feedback be pointing to inherited limitations in my approach, not just surface-level skill gaps?

For Individuals

Life Design through Self-Knowledge – Beyond Cultural Programming

Question   **Notes**

How have I changed since beginning this journey—mentally, emotionally, and professionally?

Which of these changes reflect true transformation in how I approach life, versus simply doing more of the same with extra effort?

What boundaries or habits do I need to re-establish to protect my progress?

Are those boundaries rooted in my authentic needs, or in inherited ideas of what "healthy" should look like?

What limiting beliefs am I ready to release?

<u>Question</u>   **<u>Notes</u>**

Which beliefs might be signals that certain cultural patterns or expectations need to be challenged, not just "mindset-fixed"?

How am I integrating recent learnings into my daily routines and relationships?

Does that integration show up as a different way of living and relating, or is it simply a more efficient version of my old patterns?

What would it look like to fully honor my growth and take the next aligned step?

Does my definition of "honoring my growth" reflect my genuine values, or someone else's picture of success?

Now that you've reflected across all four lenses above, it's time to zoom out again. The questions you just answered aren't random prompts; they're a snapshot into your personal data. They reveal where you're aligned, where you have drifted, and where you're being invited to grow next.

Before you move on, pause and pull the thread:

- What pattern repeated?
- What gaps are impossible to avoid, now that you have seen them?
- How would your future self thank your present self, if you were to stop settling for "how it's always been"?

Use the questions below to continue unpacking what you have uncovered into one clear snapshot of your current **S.P.A.R.K. Framework™** journey. Use these learnings to paint a picture of the next version of yourself you are ready to step into. Use it to define your work that you're ready to continue rising into.

Higher Reflection Summary Table

Question	Notes
Where in my **S.P.A.R.K.** journey do I feel strongest right now?	
Which pillar—**[S]**trategy, **[P]**lanning, **[A]**ction, **[R]**esults, or **[K]**PI Knowledge—feels most underdeveloped or neglected?	
What parts of my current plan, goals, or direction no longer align with who I am and what I value now?	
Which "strengths" might be sophisticated versions of inherited, outdated approaches I'm finally ready to release?	
Where am I feeling the most resistance? Is this a sign of necessary evolution rather than a problem to avoid?	
What is one concrete revision I can make (to my strategy, plan, actions, results tracking, or knowledge systems) in the next 30 days?	

The ones who are redefining their industries are doing more than just reflecting. They are the ones who dare to challenge any inherited framework that others would simply accept as a permanent reality. They strive to develop informed, internal knowledge-based systems that support long-term transformation versus incremental improvement that is bound by limiting structures.

This is the crossroads you're standing at right now.

You get to make a decision to either keep an outdated internal leadership playbook or rise to change it for the better.

What would it look like if you were able to leave behind or restructure inherited frameworks? What would your company look like if you were to stop chasing short-term fixes you call wins? Is it more work in the process? It absolutely is. But with it comes a legacy that lasts and pivots with each generation. When you question what you've been handed, you upgrade the internal systems you've been leading from and invite expert guidance to help you navigate those internal systems. This gives you a chance to build something new and something repeatable that works.

You don't have to overhaul everything overnight. You just have to *decide* that "how it's always been" is no longer the ceiling for who you, your team, and your organization can become. Together, you start small. One framework at a time. One internal system at a time. One aligned decision at a time.

That's how industries shift. That's how organizational cultures heal.

In the process, you just might find that you grow into the leader you are seeking to be. Why? Because you had the courage to transform broken internal systems, despite the barriers you had to face. Will you face pushback? I am sure of it. But as we close this chapter, I want to remind you: Resistance isn't a sign you're failing—it's a sign you're *leading with intention and purpose.*

When you meet that resistance with both a clear business case and a human-centered response, you build something deeper than agreement. You build deep-rooted trust that lives internally and externally. You show your team, peers, and leaders that your direction isn't about forcing change for change's sake. Instead, it's about building internal systems that support and serve the humans who live inside them every day (*your team of professionals*). That's why sustainable transformation matters. The point is not to host sharper arguments, but to cultivate respectful conversations that challenge the status quo and "norms" that no longer serve us. It is time to go beyond metrics and be organizations and individuals who include empathy into the daily experience of work. We have a chance to elevate a sense of partnership with each stakeholder in our organization and community. This is exactly what the **S.P.A.R.K. Framework™** will continue to help you do as you live out an expression of how redefined leadership lives.

So, let's make **[K]**PI Knowledge practical.

As a leader and as a human, you already know there will be concerns about your initiatives from other leaders, stakeholders, boards, decision-makers, partners, and even your own inner critic. Terms like: "budget constraints," "not the right time," "we tried that before," and "this is just how things work here." All of which tend to pop up any time change is introduced. Many of those responses sound rational, but often, they're just old leadership mindsets, approaches, patterns and internal systems protecting themselves from necessary change that hasn't occurred yet but is needed.

To help you navigate each conversation that ushers back against you, I want to leave you with a guide below. It is designed to help you respond differently to "detractors."

For each form of resistance, we will unpack:

- What it sounds like on the surface.
- How to respond with a clear business case.
- How to respond with a grounded human-centered case, honoring the people, this decision will impact (*professionals and consumers*).

Use it as a quick reference the next time you bump into "no," "not now," "we don't have the budget" or "maybe later." Let it encourage you to rise, knowing deep down that this specific type of transformation can't wait.

What Resistance Sounds Like...	How to Respond as a Leader (Business Case)	How to Respond as a Human Serving Humans
"We don't have time for this change."	Connect change to *time* by highlighting *ROI*. Show how current systems create rework, burnout, delays, and missed opportunities. Quantify the cost of "staying the same" over the next 6–12 months.	Acknowledge reality, say, "I know everyone is stretched." Then name the truth: "I don't want us to stay this exhausted. This change is about giving us a healthier, more sustainable way to work."
"We've always done it this way."	Use data and patterns. Show how "the way we've always done it" limits revenue, innovation, retention, or impact. Position the shift as risk *mitigation*, not just "innovation."	Honor history without staying stuck, say, "What got us here matters—and it's okay to admit it won't get us where we're going next." Invite feedback, ask, "What feels scary about doing this differently?"
"People will push back or won't like it."	Frame resistance as *predictable* and plan for it. Build a change roadmap that includes communication, training, and feedback loops. Show examples which highlight how pushback led to better solutions.	Normalize emotion, say, "It makes sense that people feel unsure. Change always impacts identity." Listen deeply, reflect back what you hear, and co-create small experiments instead of forcing overnight adoption.
"This will hurt our numbers."	Bring a **S.P.A.R.K.**-aligned lens to [R]esults. Model short-term vs. long-term impact. Show how sustainable internal system shifts protect revenue, reputation, and talent over time.	Speak to what people truly care about, including job security, pride in their work, feeling safe and respected. Let them know, "Our goal is not to harm performance—it's to protect our people *and* our future."
"This is just a trend / DEI / AI hype."	Reposition the concern in terms of *risk and relevance*. Show industry benchmarks, client expectations,	Bring it back to serving humans. Let them know, "This isn't about chasing trends. It's about building a place where

What Resistance Sounds Like…	How to Respond as a Leader (Business Case)	How to Respond as a Human Serving Humans
	and regulatory or market shifts. Tie the change into staying competitive and credible.	people can thrive and where we serve our communities with integrity." Welcome input by asking, "What would feel authentically us?"
"I'm not sure this will work."	Treat doubt as a design question, not a roadblock. Propose pilots, clear success criteria, and defined review dates. Emphasize test-and-learn, not all-or-nothing.	Validate vulnerability. Let them know, "Thank you for saying that out loud." Invite partnership. Say, "Let's test this together in a way that feels responsible and aligned with our values."
Silent resistance (nods in meetings, no follow-through in practice).	Look at [**K**]PI Knowledge. Observe behaviors, missed deadlines, and stalled projects. Address unclear expectations, misaligned incentives, and fear of consequences. Reset roles, rewards, and accountability.	Have real conversations. Host 1:1 check-ins, anonymous feedback, and ask honest questions like, "What's making this hard to support?" or "What do you need to feel safer or more supported in this change?"

When framed correctly, resistance isn't the end of the conversation, it's the beginning of a deeper one.

Every objection we just walked through carries an opportunity to lead with the **S.P.A.R.K. Framework™** instead of shrinking back into "how we've always done it." When you meet resistance with clarity, compassion, and a grounded business case, it bridges both impact and human-centered focus. You stop arguing for your limitations and barriers and begin to start advocating for the internal systems, organizational culture, and future you believe in. You won't win every debate. You won't influence every stakeholder overnight, but you *will* spark a shift from fear to curiosity, from delay to movement, from "prove it" to "let's explore it." Over time, those shifts compound into trust, alignment, and permission to build what's next, before your competitors do.

This is what re-defined leadership requires:

- Not perfection, but real progress and true presence.
- Not control, but courage to stand up and take on challenges.
- Not performance, but mutually beneficial and purposeful partnerships that last.

Before we proceed, let's revisit what you've learned. I welcome you to pause and embark on a reflection exercise that asks: *What limitations have you already* transformed?

After all, you are not a job title on a badge or a recommendation on LinkedIn. You are a whole human who carries responsibilities and relationships in multiple arenas at once—at work, at home, in the boardroom, at the kitchen table, with your team, with your clients, with your families, in your community, and even with yourself. The role of leadership does not only happen when giving performance reviews or designing project plans, it also happens during bedtime stories, hard conversations, big decisions, silent prayers, group texts, and the moments you choose not to give up on yourself. Every day, whether you feel it or not, you get to design a life where all of your roles, identities, and experiences intersect to shape who you are now and the legacy you are carving out to keep and what parts to leave behind you.

Outdated leadership models taught us to hide that truth. We were told to put on a "professional" mask, compartmentalize our lives, and pretend we are one person at work and another everywhere else, but let's be honest: Others can feel the disconnect. They sense when you're performing instead of embodying who you authentically are. Over time, that mask doesn't just exhaust you—it erodes trust, respect, and real impact.

The **S.P.A.R.K. Framework™** welcomes you to remove the façade and embrace full, human leadership. No mask. No fake. No fluff. You live as an aligned, honest, whole person. This full you integrates your values, story, internal systems, and vision. It is your new standard—and it is one that is universally desired by the world that exists today.

After all, this authenticity is what today's professionals and consumers are demanding of one another. They want leaders who are real, present, and courageous enough to lead as humans—not characters. These individuals know: They are not a liability to hide. They hold power to lead well.

To see how far you have come, the following exercise guides you through reflecting on each part of yourself and how you are integrating them. These lenses include:

- **You as a whole human**—This includes your inner life, well-being, identity, and relationships.
- **You as a leader** (at work and home)—This includes any place you influence others formally or informally.
- **Your Organization / Team**—This includes how your group, department, or company is evolving.
- **Your Clients / Coaching / Consulting**—This includes how you serve, guide, and create transformation for others.

Your roles may shift, overlap, and blur. That's not a problem—in fact that's the point. Use each portion below as a worksheet which helps you to process. Take your time. You don't have to fill in every box. Simply begin where it feels right for you.

Me as a whole human (My inner life, well-being, identity, and relationships)

<u>Reflection Question</u>	<u>My Notes</u>
In the last 30 days, what is one win I'm genuinely proud of?	

Reflection Question	**My Notes**
In the last 7 days, when did I feel most aligned with who I truly am?	____________________
What has drained me in my daily life more than it should?	____________________
What internal routine, boundary, or practice is currently serving me well?	____________________
What internal routine, boundary, or habit is clearly not working anymore?	____________________
Where do I feel the most momentum or excitement in my life right now?	____________________
Where do I feel stuck, hesitant, or avoidant about taking my next step?	____________________
What is one outdated pattern I'm finally ready to release?	____________________
What is one aligned step I want to take next?	____________________

Me as a Leader (At work and home)

Reflection Question	**My Notes**
In the last 30 days, what is one leadership win I'm proud of?	____________________
In the last 7 days, when did I lead in a way that felt most aligned with my values?	____________________
Where have I recently felt the most drained or stretched as a leader?	____________________
What leadership behavior or rhythm is serving my team or family well?	____________________

Reflection Question   **My Notes**

What leadership habit or pattern is no
longer working for the people I lead?   ___________________________

Where do I feel momentum or
possibility in my leadership right now?   ___________________________

Where do I feel stuck, hesitant, or afraid
to take my next leadership step?   ___________________________

What is one outdated leadership
approach I'm ready to release?   ___________________________

What is one aligned leadership action I
want to commit to taking next?   ___________________________

My Organization / Team

Reflection Question   **My Notes**

In the last 30 days, what is one meaningful
win our team or organization discovered?   ___________________________

In the last 7 days, where did our team feel
most aligned with our shared purpose?   ___________________________

What feels most draining or frustrating in
how our team/organization operates?   ___________________________

What internal system, process, or rhythm
is authentically serving our people and   ___________________________
mission?

What internal system, process, or "norm"
is not working?   ___________________________

Where do we have momentum or
opportunity as a team/organization?   ___________________________

Reflection Question   **My Notes**

Where do we feel stuck or hesitant to
move forward—even though we know we ______________________________________
need to?

What is one outdated pattern we're ready
to retire?   ______________________________________

What is one aligned step we could take
next to move toward healthier internal   ______________________________________
systems?

My Clients / Coaching / Consulting

Reflection Question   **My Notes**

In the last 30 days, what is one client or
stakeholder win I'm proud to have   ______________________________________
contributed to?

In the last 7 days, when did my work
alongside clients feel most aligned with my ______________________________________
values and purpose?

What has felt draining or misaligned in
how I currently deliver my services or   ______________________________________
support?

What part of my client experience or
delivery model is working well?   ______________________________________

What part of my client experience or
delivery model is no longer sustainable or ______________________________________
aligned?

Where do I feel momentum or possibility
when it comes to my clients, offers, or   ______________________________________
impact?

<u>Reflection Question</u>   **<u>My Notes</u>**

Where do I feel stuck, hesitant, or unsure
about my next move when it comes to my
clients or offers?

What is one outdated client or business
pattern I'm ready to release?

What is one aligned step I want to take
next to deepen my impact or refine how I
serve?

Common Patterns & Overlaps I'm Noticing

Pattern or Theme I See Repeating	The Roles It Shows Up In	What This Reveals About My Next Step

As you move through these tables, themes will echo across multiple roles. That's not a flaw, it's a fingerprint. Those patterns show you exactly where your transformation is ready to unfold.

Now that you've identified your patterns, ask yourself:

- Where do you feel the strongest right now?
- Where would you like to revisit or revise your approach?
- What parts of your plan no longer align with your current purpose?
- What approaches are you ready to release?

Remember that there is grace in this process. The goal is not to be perfect. It's to be honest and to find a way to sound like you in every space you hold.

After all, the world doesn't need a polished performance or a "perfect" leader. It needs the most aligned, grounded, unapologetic version of who you've always been and who you're becoming next. This exercise is simply a mirror and a map to help you rediscover that version of you.

This is what the future is demanding of you. In the next chapter, we'll turn that demand into a practical, **S.P.A.R.K.**-driven way of reaching it every day.

Quote to Close the Chapter:

"Metrics go deeper than the surface—wisdom sustains it. Reflect deeply, refine boldly, and re-ignite your leadership with clarity, not F.E.A.R.

— Dr. Michelle Brown

Next Up: Chapter 9 – Leading with S.P.A.R.K.: A Leadership Model That Lasts

You've done the work to name what's real, track what matters most, and learn how to face resistance without shrinking back. You've discovered what it means to create movement from inherited internal systems to intentional ones, from fear-driven reactions to informed, human-centered decisions.

Next, we're going to raise the stakes.

In the coming chapter, we'll take everything you've reflected on, tested, and tracked and turn it into a leadership identity you embody in every conversation, meeting, and room you enter. We'll explore what it looks like to lead with the **S.P.A.R.K. Framework™** as your internal operating system. You will know how to bring it with you in boardrooms and break rooms, in crisis and in calm, with your team and your family, your clients, and yourself.

Chapter 9 is where **S.P.A.R.K.** stops being "a leadership framework" and becomes the way you live and move.

CHAPTER 9 – LEADING WITH S.P.A.R.K.
A Leadership Model That Lasts

Thus far in our journey, we have discovered that leading with **S.P.A.R.K.** means leading from the inside out. More importantly, it means systematically replacing inherited leadership limitations with sustainable alternatives that create both individual fulfillment and organizational effectiveness.

We have learned that:

1. **[S]**trategy challenges inherited assumptions about what's possible rather than just optimizing performance within existing limitations.
2. **[P]**lanning gives you structure. Planning creates adaptive frameworks rather than rigid schedules. It honors both individual authenticity and organizational effectiveness.
3. **[A]**ction gives you momentum. Action systematically transforms outdated approaches rather than just implementing better tactics within familiar frameworks.
4. **[R]**esults give you reflection. Results measure transformation rather than just performance, and systematic change rather than just activity improvement.
5. **[K]**PI Knowledge gives you power. KPI Knowledge challenges inherited limitations rather than just documenting experience. This creates systematic intelligence rather than just collecting information.

All five pillars together give you impact you can revise and repeat. It offers you the chance to pass on something that lasts for future generational leaders to come. With all five pillars integrated systematically, they create leadership approaches that transform entire industries rather than just improve individual departments, teams, or organizations.

At this stage in our journey, we take everything you've done so far and shift it from being "work you did in a book" into becoming how you live and lead. This is where the **S.P.A.R.K. Framework™** shifts from just "another leadership model or a framework you reference", into a leadership identity you embody, holistically, both inside and outside of the workplace. This is where your **[S]**trategy, **[P]**lanning, **[A]**ction, **[R]**esults, and **[K]**PI Knowledge stop sitting in separate boxes and begin to work together as your streamlined internal leadership operating system.

The world doesn't need more leaders who can simply talk about change. It needs leaders who *are* the change. These leaders can walk into complexity, disruption, and discomfort and still lead from respectful and informed clarity, instead of fear-based responses and tactics. These are the leaders who dare to look at patterns handed to them and go beyond "that's how it's always been done." Such leaders are willing to redesign the internal systems, organizational cultures, and expectations others placed on them, and go beyond quietly enduring just to keep a seat at the table.

This chapter is your activation point.

You've done the reflection, you've named the gaps, and you've seen where your old leadership patterns are out of sync with the future you're called to build. Now it's time to rise into human-centered, future-focused and aligned leadership.

You are not here to maintain the status quo. You are here to interrupt it and challenge it.

Now is your time to redefine what leadership looks like in your world, whether that is at home, at work, in your team, with your clients, or in any room you step into. After all, leadership is not a buzzword or just another initiative. Before we begin, I want to be clear: Not everything from the past was wrong. Many of the practices, models, and internal systems that got us here were exactly what was needed *for that time*. They created stability, structures we could build from, and success in eras that required predictability and control. However, what once served as a foundation has now become a concrete ceiling. Sadly, many of us have held on for far too long. The very approaches that once protected us are now costing us our top talent, internal and external trust, innovation, and relevance.

The choice is no longer "change or stay the same." It's "evolve with intention or get left behind by a world that already has."

This is where the **S.P.A.R.K. Framework™** redefines leadership. It unapologetically challenges the inherited assumptions about authority, influence, and organizational effectiveness, *while* building sustainable alternatives that work for the humans inside your organizations and the communities you serve (*human consumers*). It's leadership that creates lasting impact instead of just maintaining comfortable power structures at the expense of others.

The world has changed, and leadership must, too!

We've moved beyond the predictable environments and neatly stacked hierarchies that worked when markets were slower and expectations were simpler. We are beyond the command-and-control approaches that might have kept order at one point in history, but now suffocate innovation, creativity, and human potential.

Such inherited leadership approaches aren't just outdated; they are actively counterproductive and work against you. We must shift toward an environment that carries agility, courage, collaboration, and authentic human engagement without the mask or fluff.

This is your invitation—and your responsibility—to rise.

To make this practical and bring this full circle, let's look at how outdated leadership models compare to what the world is demanding from us now.

Outdated Leadership vs. New Era Leadership

Category	Outdated Leadership Models / Thinking	New Era Leadership Models / Thinking
Leader Identity	I am my title. My authority comes from my position, and I need to look like I have it all together.	I am a whole human who leads wherever I am. My authority comes from my integrity, impact, and how I treat people.
Power & Control	Power is about control. I make the decisions, others execute. Being "in charge" means being untouchable.	Power is shared. I set direction and create conditions where others can lead, contribute, and grow. Being "in charge" means being accountable and accessible.
Communication	Information is on a need-to-know basis. People should do what they're told without needing the full picture.	Communication is transparent and two-way. People deserve context, clarity, and a voice in how we move forward.
Performance & Results	As long as the numbers look good, everything is fine. People are replaceable; results are not.	Results and people are inseparable. Sustainable performance matters more than short-term spikes that burn people out or break trust.
Humanity & Emotion	Feelings don't belong at work. "Professional" means neutral, distant, and always "fine."	Emotions are data. People bring their whole selves to work. Naming genuine obstacles helps us lead wisely and support each other better.
Change & Uncertainty	Change is a threat. Our job is to protect how things have always been and avoid disruption.	Change is constant. Our job is to adapt with intention, learn quickly, and use disruption as a catalyst for better ways to work and serve.
Mistakes & Accountability	Mistakes equal failure. They must be hidden or punished. Blame keeps me safe.	Mistakes are learning opportunities. We own our impact, repair where needed, and improve the systems that created the issue in the first place.
Diversity & Inclusion	Diversity is a checkbox. We do the minimum to look compliant and avoid controversy.	Diversity, equity, and inclusion are non-negotiable. We design our culture, decisions, and internal systems so that more people can belong, contribute, and thrive.
Development & Growth	Development is for a chosen few at the top. Everyone else should be grateful to have a job.	Development is for everyone. We invest in people at all levels and expect leaders to grow just as much as their teams.
Self-Image as a Leader	I need to be seen as an expert with all the answers. Admitting "I don't know" would reveal weakness.	I am a learner and a guide. I ask better questions, bring in better voices, and co-create better answers.

If you've felt the tension between these two columns, you're not alone.

This is exactly the gap the world is demanding organizations face. Sadly, it is the gap most organizational leaders also choose to ignore. But the **S.P.A.R.K. Framework™** was born to bridge such a gap. For you see, the **S.P.A.R.K. Framework™** weaves "new era" expectations into a holistic model you can actually live out daily through created habits, not just admire on the page.

To begin, let's honor what worked in the past, release what no longer does, and lead with *"new era"* expectations that honor you as a fully integrated human being, one who leads authentically.

Traditional vs New-Era Leadership Through the Lens of S.P.A.R.K.

S.P.A.R.K. Pillar	Outdated Leadership Approach	New-Era / S.P.A.R.K.-Aligned Leadership
[S]trategy	Strategy is a static document, built to impress others and rarely revisited.	[S]trategy is a living compass that guides decisions and remains anchored to values and purpose.
[P]lanning	Planning is rigid, top-down, and disconnected from real life.	[P]lanning is adaptive, honest, and co-created with the people who must enact it.
[A]ction	Action means staying busy, saying yes to everything, and glorifying urgency.	[A]ction means taking fewer, clearer, braver steps that move you toward the end goal.
[R]esults	Results are measured by short-term numbers and external optics.	[R]esults include people, culture, sustainability, and long-term impact, not just profit.
[K]PI Knowledge	KPIs are inherited, unquestioned, and used to justify old decisions.	[K]PI Knowledge is intentionally chosen, regularly questioned, and used to learn, refine, and evolve.

Here's the truth:

Anyone can lead when things are going smoothly.

And….Anyone can manage within inherited systems, "when" those internal systems are functioning adequately.

But true leadership shows up when things truly shift, when people are uncertain, when internal systems are challenged, and the future feels unclear and uncertain. True leadership shows up when inherited approaches reach their limits and systematic transformation becomes necessary for survival and success. That's when the **S.P.A.R.K. Framework™** shines. That's when leaders who have developed systematic intelligence, rather than just management skills, become catalysts for possibilities no one thought was possible.

Here's the point, this isn't optional anymore, it's a must! Thriving in today's world requires leaders who are adaptable, authentic, and systemically transformative as the human beings they are.

> *Here's the hard truth:*
>
> *If you don't make this shift, your competitors will.*
>
> *The companies willing to lead in such an innovative way will become the places where your top talent goes to grow and where your most value-driven consumers choose to spend, stay, and refer other consumers too.*

Let's take a peek at what is required of leadership in this new era.

Leading: Then vs. Now

Category	Traditional Leadership (Then)	Redefined Era of Leadership (Now)
Defining Characteristic	Command and Control	Influence and Empowerment
Communication Style	Top-Down, One-Way	Open, Transparent, Two-Way
Motivation Approach	Fear-Based, Punitive	Purpose-Driven, Empathetic
Focus	Technical Skills, Rules	Soft Skills, Well-Being
Succession Planning	Replicate the Current Leader	Cultivates Diverse, Authentic Leaders
Reaction to Change	Rigid, Slow	Agile, Adaptive, Fact-Based, Fluid

Now that you've experienced each pillar of the **S.P.A.R.K. Framework™—[S]**trategy, **[P]**lanning, **[A]**ction, **[R]**esults, **and [K]**PI Knowledge—you're ready to lead with it.

Not just apply it, not just teach it, but embody it.

Consider the transformation of Dr. Angela Martinez, CEO of a healthcare system, who faced the challenge of leading through industry-wide disruption while maintaining quality patient care and staff morale. Traditional healthcare leadership approaches focus on crisis management, cost containment, and regulatory compliance.

Their goal is to essentially optimize performance within inherited healthcare delivery models. However, Dr. Martinez recognized that her industry challenges weren't management problems. They could not be solved with better execution of existing approaches. Instead, her team faced systematic problems that required core transformation of how healthcare leadership functions during complexity. Therefore, they brought in third-part guidance.

Recognizing when to bring in an expert to shift internal systems and alter outdated decision-making barriers ensures that organizations will not just implement better management practices. Instead, they have a chance to systematically transform how leadership operates by using streamlined and aligned strategies. This includes updating approaches, policies, procedures—along with re-structuring enterprise-wide trainings. Instead of hierarchical decision-making during crisis, they create collaborative intelligence networks. This means includes voices such as cross-functional groups of clinicians, operational leaders, data experts, and frontline staff. Such a collaboration of experts are able to share real-time information, test solutions quickly, and make decisions within clear, quality guardrails. These networks are able to adapt rapidly to changing conditions while still honoring safety protocols, regulatory requirements, and evidence-based standards of care. Collaborative intelligence networks do not compete for resources across departments. They create integrated value creation approaches that strengthen the entire internal ecosystem. Instead of reacting to industry changes, they begin anticipating and influencing industry evolution.

By using this approach, Dr. Angela was able to:

- Redefine leadership in her region and industry.
- Build outcomes that improved while her costs decreased.
- The staff in her organization reported staff engagement levels soared as professionals felt empowered to innovate rather than just comply. They were able to do more than *"check the box"* or *"quietly quit, collect their check, then go home."*
- Most importantly, her team created a *standard* that other organizations begin to study and replicate within their leadership models and practices. Once more, this proved that internal system transformation of leadership approaches ignites industry-wide change.

Consider the growth that Robert Chen, Chief Technology Officer at a major energy corporation, experienced when he faced the challenge of leading technological innovation while also navigating industry transformation and regulatory complexity. Traditional technology leadership in energy focuses on operational efficiency, risk management, and incremental innovations. It essentially asks teams to optimize inherited technology approaches rather than transforming them.

Robert recognized that their technology challenges weren't implementation problems that could be solved with better project management. Instead, they were internal system problems that required fundamental transformation of how technology leadership functions in complex, evolving industries.

By partnering with an external expert, organizations don't just upgrade technology systems; they systematically transform how technology leadership operates throughout their corporation. Instead of siloed technology development, they create integrated ecosystems that connect technology advancement with business strategy. There is room for environmental responsibility to work in tandem with professional goals that exist within updated HR practices and community impact. Instead of reactive compliance with industry standards, Robert's team begin proactively developing technological approaches that influence industry evolution.

The transformation they experienced positioned their corporation as a technology leader rather than a technology adopter. Why does this matter? Because innovation cycles accelerate while implementation risks decrease. Cross-functional collaboration improves dramatically as technology development becomes integrated with overall business transformation. Most importantly, their technological leadership model becomes the standard that other companies begin studying and adopting.

Robert's team shows us critical wins that many of us can learn from. Consider how they:

1. Operate from reassured clarity and confidence, not confusion. Their clarity came from systematic intelligence rather than inherited assumptions. Their confidence came from proven transformation results rather than a pile of accumulated experience.
2. Drive team and culture by modeling adaptability. They are grounded in systematic principles rather than reactive pivoting. Their culture development is based on authentic values rather than inherited organizational patterns.
3. Create sustainable systems that outlast any one person or position. Their systems continuously evolve and improve rather than just maintain stability. Their sustainability is based on systematic transformation principles rather than just efficient operations.
4. Balance business outcomes with human-centered and people-first strategies. This balance integrates rather than compromises. The strategies they used enhanced both business effectiveness and human fulfillment rather than treating them as competing priorities.

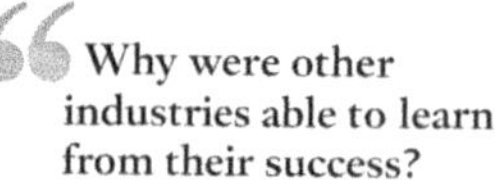

Because the S.P.A.R.K. Framework™ *is universal and adaptable.*

It addresses the **internal system challenges** that limit leadership effectiveness— rather than just providing *better tactics for managing within existing limitations.*

It doesn't require perfection. Its intentionality aligns with progress. *It doesn't force transformation; it supports it.*

It doesn't demand that leaders abandon their **authentic strengths**; *it helps them express those strengths through informed approaches that create* **lasting impact**— *rather than just temporary improvements.*

—Dr. Michelle Brown, The S.P.A.R.K. Framework Effect – Redefining Leadership

This form of refinement creates transformation rather than just improvement within existing limitations. I would encourage you to apply such learnings to your personal and professional life, team meetings, goal-setting sessions, performance reviews, and your own self-reflection rituals. It is a comprehensive framework that integrates individual development with organizational evolution, personal authenticity with professional effectiveness.

So what does a **S.P.A.R.K. Framework™**-centered leader look like in practice?

A **S.P.A.R.K. Framework™**-centered leader operates from reassured clarity and confidence, not confusion.

That clarity comes from fully developed internal systems which have given them significant systematic intelligence. They know how to consistently gather, interpret, and act on information across their internal systems, not from gut feelings or old habits.

Systematic intelligence includes regular reflection, clear KPIs, honest feedback, and continuous review of patterns, both internally and externally as well as personally and professionally. They act on these things on purpose, not just when something breaks. Their confidence doesn't come from title or tenure alone; it comes from *evidence* that their choices are creating transformation. They go beyond motion and define movement.

They drive team and organizational culture by modeling adaptability that's grounded in systematic principles, not reaction. What are these *systematic principles*? They are the non-negotiables that guide how they lead. These include clear values, decision rules, and internal standards they return to when things get hard. Instead of pivoting based on pressure, trends, or the loudest voice in the room, they ask, *"What do our values, our strategy, and our data tell us?"*

Then they adjust from there.

We all know that organizational culture doesn't shift because of speeches; it shifts because people repeatedly see meaningful principles in action. When a leader creates sustainable internal systems, they outlast any one person or position. Such a repeatable way of working is a gift. It lets the team know that our processes, agreements, and rhythms don't depend on one heroic leader to hold everything together. Let's be honest, that's not realistic. From there, collective ownership guides growth.

From here:

- One-time wins, become shared workflows.
- Individuals document "how we do this," so others can carry it forward.
- There is room to build check-ins, feedback loops, and clear ownership into the way work actually happens.

Such internal systems are designed to evolve and improve, not just maintain stability. The company grows with the market and in doing so, becomes steady. Sustainability, in this context, means your organization can keep growing and adapting *without* burning people out or collapsing every time someone leaves. There is a natural balance of business outcomes, paired with human-centered and people-first strategies.

Leaders refuse the false choice between "hit the numbers" and "care for the humans." Instead, they design internal systems where each can coexist. Within the organization's culture, performance, well-being, innovation, and inclusion for all, this now becomes a part of the ecosystem and how decisions are made, how work is structured, and how success is measured in a streamlined way.

These leaders ask:

"How do we reach our goals in a way that people can live with and grow from, over time?

Just in case you are asking, "But what if I'm not a CEO? How can "*I*" lead like this?" Let me assure you.

You don't have to be a CEO to lead this way. You can be a team member, a coach, a parent, or an aspiring changemaker. Leadership is not a job title—it's influence plus intention.

Leading with the **S.P.A.R.K. Framework™** in any role, no matter the level, might look like:

- Turning one chaotic process into a simple checklist or shared template everyone can use (repeatedly).
- Running regular, honest retros where your team can tell the truth about what is and isn't working and using that input to refine your internal systems.
- Helping clients move from "trying everything" to a focused, values-aligned **S.P.A.R.K. Framework™** plan, they can sustain and repeat.
- Tracking your own habits, boundaries, and energy like data. Then adjusting how you work and live, not from shame, but from self-respect.

When I encourage others to "*rise with intention,*" I am not advocating for us to suddenly become perfect or fearless. I mean leading on purpose instead of on autopilot. It's about making a defined and determined choice and choosing to move towards leadership daily.

It means taking the opportunity to address:

- One conversation you won't avoid.
- One boundary you will honor.
- One chance to speak up and stand for something that matters.
- One internal system you will improve instead of complain about.

That's how systematic transformation starts. It is always rooted in small, consistent steps that compound over time. In turn, these create embedded daily habits that eventually become the natural essence of who you are.

Use the **S.P.A.R.K. Framework™** not as a one-time process. It's a leadership compass and new ecosystem which allows you to:

- Revisit **[S]**trategy when your reality or goals shift.
- Refine **[P]**lanning so it matches current capacity, not fantasy.
- Align **[A]**ction with what matters most right now.
- Measure **[R]**esults in ways that reflect human beings *and* performance.
- Build **[K]**PI Knowledge that turns lived experience into wisdom you can re-use.

My advice? Revisit each pillar regularly. Go back to any pillar as many times as you need to stay aligned with your desired end goals. Apply it to your personal and professional life. Use it in team meetings, goal-setting sessions, performance reviews, and your own self-reflection rituals. Apply it as a framework for transformation that integrates individual development with organizational evolution, personal authenticity with professional effectiveness.

That's what a **S.P.A.R.K. Framework™**-centered leader looks like. None of us have to be someone who has it all figured out. All we must do is rise to become someone who is committed to evolving our internal systems, on purpose, for the good of the human beings we serve and the future we are building both personally and professionally.

S.P.A.R.K. Pillar	When You Know It's Time to Come Back to This Pillar	Ask Yourself...	Simple Ways to Re-Align (Personally & Professionally)
[S]trategy	You feel pulled in a hundred directions and say yes to everything. Yet you are not sure what any of it is building toward. Your team or family keeps asking, "What's the real priority?"	*"What truly matters most in this season—for me, my team, and the people I serve?"*	Rename your 1–3 core priorities for this season.
[P]lanning	Your days feel chaotic. You're busy all day, every day. But by the end of the week you are wondering what you actually pushed forward. Firefighting wins over focused work.	*"Does my current week match what I say my priorities are?"*	Take one big priority and break it into 3–5 concrete steps. Communicate your plan with key people so expectations are clear.
[A]ction	You're stuck in analysis, overthinking and waiting for the "perfect moment." You keep refining the plan but do not move towards enacting it.	*"What is one aligned step I can take in the next 24–48 hours?"*	Choose one small, low-resistance action that supports your end goal and complete it within two days. Let completion—not size—be the win.
[R]esults	You feel unsure if anything you're doing is "working." You see activity, but you can't tell if there's progress or it is all meaningless motion.	*"How do I know whether my plan is truly working—for me, my team, and those we serve?"*	Pick 2–3 indicators that matter most (e.g., energy, engagement, completion of key milestones, trust, impact on others, etc.). Review them. If you don't like what you see, adjust.
[K]PI Knowledge	You keep repeating the same lessons. Challenges look different on the surface but feel strangely familiar. Wins pass by without being captured or repeated.	*"What did this season teach me that I never want to forget?"*	After critical weeks, projects, or life moments, pause to reflect and take notes on your observations (this is your data).

Now that you've had a chance to find patterns and have identified any obstacles in your **S.P.A.R.K. Framework™** journey, let's go a level deeper. The following set of questions will help you apply what you've recognized. This is your chance to process where you are in your journey. It is your moment to assess how the **S.P.A.R.K. Framework™** is present in your leadership identity. From here, your answers will guide you in moving forward as you become a catalyst for systematic transformation.

S.P.A.R.K. Framework™ Leadership Reflection

Embodying the Framework Beyond Inherited Leadership Limitations

For Organizations & Teams

How do we ensure our strategy is understood and practiced at every level?

____

____

Does our strategy represent a systematic transformation of industry approaches or is it just a way to improve execution within our inherited organizational frameworks?

____

____

What systems have we implemented that support ongoing planning and progress?

____

____

Do these systems include adaptive transformation capacity or are they simply better management of inherited organizational patterns?

____

____

How consistently do we take aligned action—and where do we stall?

____

____

Does our "alignment" reflect authentic organizational values or are they inherited assumptions about what effective organizational action should look like?

What organizational results are we most proud of this year?

Do these results represent systematic transformation of organizational effectiveness or are they a result of improved performance within inherited operational frameworks?

How do we build knowledge-sharing into our daily operations?

Does our knowledge-sharing challenge any of our inherited organizational assumptions or do they simply document and spread familiar approaches more effectively?

For Leaders

What **S.P.A.R.K.** Pillar do I lead most confidently—and why?

Does my confidence come from the systematic mastery of transformation principles or do I simply have improved skills within inherited leadership frameworks?

Where do I need to grow to lead with greater intention?

Does this growth area represent systematic transformation opportunities or just skill development within familiar leadership patterns?

What has shifted in my leadership style since using the **S.P.A.R.K. Framework™**?

Do these shifts represent systematic transformation of leadership approach or just tactical improvements within inherited management models?

What feedback have I received—and how have I responded?

Does this feedback challenge inherited leadership assumptions or just provide suggestions for improvement within familiar frameworks?

How do I support others by helping them to activate their own **S.P.A.R.K.**?

Am I helping others develop systematic transformation capacity or just improve performance within inherited development approaches?

For Coaches & Consultants

How am I applying **S.P.A.R.K.** to guide my clients with clarity and purpose?

Does my guidance create systematic transformation in how clients approach their challenges or just help them improve execution within inherited problem-solving frameworks?

Which client success stories best reflect the power of this framework?

Do these success stories demonstrate systematic transformation or just improved results within inherited limitation patterns?

Where do I need to deepen my own embodiment of **S.P.A.R.K.**?

____

____

Does this deepening represent systematic transformation of my coaching approach or is it skill refinement within inherited coaching models?

____

____

How can I better measure and communicate results to my clients?

____

____

Do my measurement approaches capture systematic transformation, or do they simply document improvement within inherited success frameworks?

____

____

What tools, offers, or insights can I refine to deliver more value?

____

____

Do these refinements represent systematic innovation in value delivery or just better execution of inherited coaching approaches?

____

____

For Individuals

Which **S.P.A.R.K.** Pillar is my personal superpower—and how do I know?

____

____

Does this superpower reflect systematic mastery of transformation principles, or does it relay that I have developed skills within inherited personal development frameworks?

____

____

What old habits or narratives have I released on this journey?

____

____

Do these releases represent systematic transformation, or are they improved management of inherited personal patterns?

____

____

Where do I still feel resistance—and how can I gently shift it?

____

____

Is this resistance protecting inherited limitations or warning against authentic transformation opportunities that challenge familiar patterns?

____

____

How am I bringing **S.P.A.R.K.** into my relationships, work, or daily life?

____

____

Does this integration represent systematic transformation or is my approach simply an improved execution within inherited lifestyle frameworks?

____

____

What one brave step I'm ready to take right now?

Does this step challenge inherited assumptions about what's possible or just push me harder within familiar limitation boundaries?

Remember:

The ***S.P.A.R.K. Framework*™** *isn't just a moment. It's a model, a map, and a movement.*

It's a systematic approach to transformation that challenges inherited limitations rather than just optimizes performance within existing outdated frameworks.

Now is our time to rise and lead a future that works for us! The world is shifting and so is the standard for current leaders and leaders of the future.

Quote to Close the Chapter:

"Reflection turns experience into insight, but what you do with that insight defines your legacy. Leaders who transform it into systematic, industry-shaping action redefine what's possible for everyone.

— Dr. Michelle Brown

Next Up: Chapter 10 – S.P.A.R.K. IGNITED™: Proof, Power, Progress

You've done the work—reflected, realigned, and recommitted. Now it's time to see the evidence. In our next chapter, we'll shift from "doing the framework" to recognizing the proof of who you've become because of the work you have put in. You'll see how the **S.P.A.R.K. Framework™** shows up as visible results in your organization, your leadership, your clients, and your own life.

Now is your chance to claim this proof as power, not by luck or chance.

CHAPTER 10 – S.P.A.R.K. IGNITED™
PROOF, POWER, PROGRESS

This chapter is your permission slip to celebrate the proof of your progress! You've strategized. You've planned and you've acted. You've measured and you've reflected. Now is the time to step into your power. This is your moment to walk boldly in your next level of leadership with clarity and conviction. This is where the **S.P.A.R.K. Framework™**, as it applies to you, is no longer internal. It's visible, embodied, and transformational.

You are the proof of redefined leadership for the future—and that future is now!

How do you know? I'm glad you asked:

<u>What It Really Means (In This Book)</u>	<u>How You'll Recognize It in Your Life & Work</u>
Proof The visible evidence that your **S.P.A.R.K. Framework™** work is real, and not theory or intention, is based on outcomes. It's what others can *see* and what you can *point to* with clarity.	• Your decisions line up with your values, even under pressure. • Your team, clients, or family note the difference in how you lead. • You can name specific wins, shifts, and breakthroughs that didn't exist before you applied the **S.P.A.R.K. Framework™**.
Power Influence does not come from ego, title, or control. Instead, it comes from grounded authority stemming from alignment, self-awareness, and lived results. It's the calm, clear confidence of someone who knows who they are and what they stand for.	• You stop shrinking, over-explaining, or waiting for permission to do what you know is right. • You make decisions from your values, not from fear or people-pleasing behaviors. • You can say "yes" and "no" with clarity and keep your peace after you do.
Progress The ongoing movement of your life, leadership, and internal systems is moving in the right direction. This is less about perfection or overnight transformation. Instead, it is rooted in consistent, intentional evolution.	• Your calendar, habits, and internal systems look like the life and leadership you state you want. • Setbacks don't send you back to zero. You know how to reset, learn, and keep going. • You can look back 30, 60, 90 days and *name* how you've grown, not just how busy you've been.

As you move through this chapter, I want you to keep three anchors in mind. You're not chasing someone else's definition of success. Instead, you're gathering proof, standing in your power, and honoring your progress. Therefore, you are a leader who is redefining what's possible for yourself and everyone you serve.

Your organization, team, clients, and life are each a reflection of the effort, alignment, and adaptability you are committed to cultivating. This is not the end; it's your expansion point. Your transformation has not concluded. It simply becomes evidence that change creates impact that reaches beyond what you initially imagined possible.

To allow the **S.P.A.R.K. Framework™** to be more than a one-time tool, we must use it as a way of leading, operating, and evolving across time. This chapter demonstrates what happens when individuals and organizations do just that. The collective **proof** isn't just in any of our individual successes—it's in the ripple effects we each have a chance to create:

- The internal systems we have challenged.
- The outdated approaches we have replaced.
- The sustainable alternatives we have built.
- The leaders we have inspired.
- The organizations we have influenced.
- The industries and teams of professionals we have helped evolve.

Does it take outside help to reach these goals and keep the **S.P.A.R.K. Framework™** alive? Yes, but that is exactly why external partners exist—to help leaders and organizations not just achieve better results, but to become catalysts for systematic transformation. As they collaborate, it creates *proof* of what's possible when authentic purpose meets strategic implementation. From here, we now shift to being *powered* by human-centered approaches that integrate with technological efficiency, which lead to results we get to see and observe how the *progress* of individual transformation drives organizational revolution.

Let's venture into various scenarios to see how these goals are set in motion for real movement. From here, we have a chance to identify our own proof, power and progress playbook based on our specific scenario.

For Organization & Teams: The Cultural Shift in Motion

Here is the Proof:

Teams no longer operate in silos; they now collaborate cross-functionally. They move forward because strategy, structure, and shared metrics now connect them in a clear and concise, streamlined manner. Teams have fundamentally transformed how work gets done. They have replaced competitive internal dynamics with collaborative value creation, outdated communication hierarchies with transparent knowledge sharing, and inherited departmental boundaries with integrated impact delivery.

This is their Power:

The organizational culture has reached a point in which physical and psychological safety, innovation, and human-centered performance are valued just as much as the ROI of the organization. Beyond valuation, the organizational culture has systematically integrated these values into every decision-making process, policy, and procedure. This includes each performance evaluation and every strategic initiative. Combined, this proves the fact that human-centered approaches don't compromise business effectiveness; they enhance it exponentially, making it powerful.

This is their Progress:

Teams realign every quarter, versus waiting until the last minute, leading to teams adjusting without panic. This allows them to lead from data and empathy. Now, beyond quarterly alignment, teams that have built adaptive internal systems that can navigate any challenge, while staying grounded in authentic purpose. They have replaced reactive crisis management with proactive opportunity creation. They become a model that other organizations study and replicate.

Consider the transformation evidence from Global Tech Solutions, a mid-sized software company that implemented the **S.P.A.R.K. Framework™** across their entire organization. Traditional metrics showed impressive results, but the real proof was found in their internal system restructurings. They had fundamentally transformed from a hierarchical, competitive culture to a collaborative, innovative ecosystem. They didn't just improve their numbers; they created a new organizational DNA.

Departments that had operated in silos for decades began co-creating solutions. Decision-making that had once been strictly top-down shifted into collaborative intelligence networks. These cross-functional groups of leaders and frontline professionals shared data, surfaced patterns, and made decisions together with the people closest to the work and the customer voice present in the room. Innovation that had once been confined to a single Research & Development department began to flow from every corner of the company: operations, HR, sales, product, and support all contributed. Together, they turned the outdated statements of "that's not my lane" mindset into "let's solve this together." In the end, they made creative problem-solving an organization-wide norm, not a specialty function. As this happened, other companies began studying their transformation model, once more proving that systematic organizational culture change creates industry influence.

The *power* wasn't rooted in their internal transformation alone; it was in their market positioning.

They became the employer of choice in their region, the preferred vendor for companies seeking collaborative partnerships, and a case study that business schools began teaching about.

Global Tech Solutions: Proof, Power, Progress Snapshot

	In Their Story	What To Look For in Your Org/Team
Proof	Departments that used to compete transformed to co-create solutions. Siloed teams shifted into a collaborative, innovative ecosystem.	Look for signs that teams are collaborating *with* each other instead of around or against each other. This often sounds like joint projects, shared wins, and fewer "us vs. them" conversations.
Power	Human-centered practices (physical and psychological safety, shared decision-making, and transparent communication) became part of how decisions were made, not just values painted on the wall.	Look for indications that "how you treat people" is built into your processes. This often is evidenced by who's in the room, how feedback is handled, and how conflicts are resolved—not just what numbers say.
Progress	Teams began realigning regularly using the **S.P.A.R.K. Framework™**. They shifted from crisis-response to proactive, cross-functional problem-solving. Other companies began studying their model.	Look for evidence that your "progress" is not masquerading as putting out fires. True progress is evidenced by regular check-ins, improved handoffs, fewer repeated breakdowns, and external stakeholders asking, "How are you all doing this?"

You don't need to overhaul your entire company to see this kind of shift.
You have a chance to start exactly where you are, ask better questions, take one aligned action at a time, and let your own version of *proof, power, and progress* surface. Slowly, these changes will become visible in the way you lead, the way your team operates, and the way your organization shows up in the world.

From Story to Strategy: How You Can Start Creating Proof, Power & Progress.

What You Want to Create	Questions to Ask Yourself / Your Team	Simple First Steps (Personally & Organizationally)
Proof – Evidence that things are *changing*, not just being talked about	• Where have we seen behaviors shift, not just policies change? • What feels different regarding how we meet, make decisions, and work together today compared to one year ago?	• Pick **one area** (meetings, cross-team projects, feedback) and list three specific "before vs. after" shifts you have noticed. • Ask 3–5 people: "What feels different about how we work now?" Capture their language as living proof.
Power – You use influence, voice, and decision-making differently now	• Whose voices are we currently heeding that we didn't hear before? • Have we shifted from select decision-makers having say to having the people closest to the work make decisions?	• Map one recurring decision (e.g., roadmap, staffing, priorities). Ask yourself: "Who used to have the final decision? Who's making that decision now?" • Add one new practice. Create a quick "frontline pulse" before carrying out a big decision—be it a survey, Slack poll, or huddles.
Progress – Momentum is sustainable versus a short-term push	• What 2–3 signs indicate we are moving forward with less chaos than before? • Where are we adjusting with intention instead of reacting in panic?	• Choose one of the **S.P.A.R.K.** Pillars to review with your team each quarter ([S]trategy, [P]lanning, [A]ction, [R]esults, or [K]PI Knowledge). • Start a simple "progress log." Once a month, initiate a team discussion to ask, "What got better? What felt easier? What did we learn?"

Now, let's look into how the proof, power, and progress indicators play out for leaders during uncertain times.

For Leaders: The Anchor in Uncertain Times

Consider the leadership evidence from Dr. Maria Santos, a Chief Executive of a major healthcare network. Dr. Santos faced the challenge of leading through industry transformation while maintaining patient care excellence. Traditional leadership metrics favored results for improved patient outcomes, increased staff satisfaction, and reduced operational costs. However, the real proof of her success was deeper and systematic. She fundamentally transformed how healthcare leadership functions during complexity by seeking to go deeper.

Dr. Santos didn't just become a better leader; she redefined what healthcare leadership could accomplish. Instead of managing crisis after crisis, she created anticipatory internal systems that prevented them. Instead of competing for resources across departments, she fostered collaborative resource optimization. Instead of reacting to industry changes, she began influencing healthcare policy and practice standards. Her power went beyond her individual effectiveness and rippled out to industry impact. As a result, other healthcare systems began adopting her leadership approaches.

Medical associations invited her to share transformation strategies. Policy makers consulted her on sustainable healthcare delivery models. This allowed her to show proof that leaders who implement the **S.P.A.R.K. Framework™** don't just succeed, they create effective, sustainable approaches you can see and feel, repeatedly.

Dr. Santos: Proof, Power, Progress Snapshot

	<u>In Her Story (Example)</u>	<u>What To Look For Within Your Leadership</u>
Proof	Patient outcomes improved, staff satisfaction rose, and operational costs decreased—*while* navigating industry disruption.	Look for hard indicators (results and human metrics) that improve at the same time (i.e. performance is up, burnout and chaos are down).
Power	She moved from crisis management to anticipatory internal systems. By seeing around corners and building structures, she prevented repeated emergencies.	Recognize the fact you are not surprised by the same problems every quarter. Note the fact you build processes, versus patch on last-minute saves.
Progress	Her leadership approach became a model. Other healthcare systems, associations, and policymakers sought her out for transformation strategies.	Look for people external to your immediate leadership scope to ask for your input, borrow your practices, or model their approach on yours. Recognize that way of leading travels further than your title.

Dr. Santos' story is powerful, but it's not meant to stay on the page. Her success is not intended to be a distant example. It's a mirror and a model for what's possible in your world. You may not be leading a healthcare network, but you *are* leading humans through seasons of complexity. The levers are the same. How you gather knowledge, share power, and turn learning into repeatable progress, matters.

Using the table below, consider how to translate her transformation into your own next steps, right where you are.

Dr. Santos – Proof, Power, Progress: How You Can Start, Too

What You Want to Create	Questions to Ask Yourself / Your Team	Simple First Steps Moves (Personally & Organizationally)
Steady leadership in uncertainty (less panic, more pivot).	When disruption hits, do I react first or pause to understand what's happening?	Commit to a brief "pause practice" before making major decisions. Take 5–10 minutes to clarify facts, risks, and values before you respond or announce a change.
Decisions rooted in values, not pressure.	Are our biggest decisions clearly connected to our stated values—or do they align to urgency, optics, and external noise?	Choose 3–5 core values and add a check-in. Ask, "How does this decision reflect each of these values?" Build that question into leadership meetings and decision templates.
Anticipatory systems versus constant crisis management.	What patterns repeat during our crises—and what are they trying to tell us about our internal systems?	After every major issue, run a short debrief. Ask, "What happened? What did we miss? "What early signals were present? What system do we need to adjust so this doesn't repeat?"
Shared leadership versus "lone wolf" leadership.	Who else needs to be at the table for this decision—and whose insight are we consistently missing?	Create a small "critical insight circle" of cross-functional voices. Tap into this group before big decisions. Rotate members so diverse perspectives shape your pivots.
A leadership presence that calms, aligns, and activates others.	How do people feel after they leave a meeting with me? Are they clear and grounded, or anxious and confused?	Ask 2–3 trusted people for honest feedback on how your communication lands. Next, set one intention per week (e.g., "end every meeting with 3 clear next steps").

These action steps show us how transformative leadership plays out at an organizational and executive level. It proves that steady leadership, anticipatory internal systems, decisions, and factual informed data results must be rooted in values, not panic.

Next, let's shift lenses to coaches and consultants. Whether you're running your own practice or serving inside an organization, the mindset is the same, however, the pivot is in how you design, deliver, and measure your impact.

For Coaches & Consultants: The Framework Behind Client Success

Here is the Proof:

Clients see measurable results not because of hustle, but because their strategy, actions, and internal systems are aligned. Beyond results, clients have systematically transformed their approach to their own challenges. They operate from authentic purpose rather than inherited limitations and create sustainable success rather than cyclical achievement.

This is their Power:

Their offers are no longer random or reactive. Instead, they are built around repeatable, customizable frameworks like the **S.P.A.R.K. Framework™**. Beyond structured offers, their systematic services and deliveries create consistent transformation results for them and their clients. In turn, this generates organic referrals through authentic value creation.

This is their Progress:

The business sustains impact without sacrificing wellness or alignment. This is a company in which both client outcomes and coach clarity are present each day. Beyond balanced success, the business integrates personal authenticity with professional excellence. Coaches scale due to systematic approaches rather than unsustainable hustle with no measurable results. In turn, this creates industry influence through transformation expertise.

Consider the consulting evidence of Jennifer Martinez, an organizational development consultant who transformed her scattered practice into a vibrant consultancy. Traditional business metrics showed remarkable growth, but her proof went deeper. She fundamentally transformed how consulting creates lasting change. Jennifer didn't just scale her business; she revolutionized her industry approach. Instead of offering generic consulting services, she developed signature methodologies. Instead of competing on price or availability, she leveraged her results. Instead of chasing every opportunity, she attracted ideal clients who were willing to put in the work of creating authentic, lasting change.

Her power did not lie in her business success; it was rooted in her client impact. Organizations that worked with her began outperforming competitors who used traditional consulting approaches. Her clients became case studies of systematic transformation, which caused other consultants to begin studying and adopting her methodologies. She proved that consultants who implement the **S.P.A.R.K. Framework™** don't just build successful practices, they elevate entire industries toward more effective, authentic service delivery.

You don't need a huge team, a fancy brand, or a viral platform to create this kind of proof, power, and progress. What Jennifer did was simple, yet intentional. She stopped guessing, stopped building from scratch every time, and started leading her work through a clear, repeatable framework.

Here's how you can begin doing the same:

What You Want to Create	Questions to Ask Yourself / Your Team	Simple First Steps (Personally & In Your Practice)
Proof – which includes clear, repeatable client results versus saying to yourself "I hope this works."	• In their words, not mine, what specific transformations do my top clients experience from me? • What current offers am I reinventing instead of using a simple, repeatable process?	• Choose your top 3 favorite client wins and write out: "Before → After → How we got there." Highlight the common steps. • Turn those common steps into a named mini framework (even if it's rough). Next, start using that language in discovery calls.
Power – which includes a framework-based offer versus depleting your energy on custom work.	• If someone asked, "What's your signature process?" could I explain it in 2–3 sentences? • Which parts of my work must be custom and what could be standardized—without losing signature service?	• Write a one-paragraph "This is how I work" explainer which defines your stages: Share it with current clients and ask for feedback. • Standardize one thing. This might be your onboarding, your first session structure, or your review/check-in rhythm.
Progress – which includes building a business that grows without burning you out in the process.	• Where am I over-giving, over-prepping, or over-customizing? How is this draining me more than helping my clients? • If my business had to run at 80% of my energy, what would I keep, simplify, or let go of?	• Do a weekly recap. Ask, "What gave me energy? What drained me? What will I do less of next week?" Adjust one thing at a time. • Choose one offer, one type of client, or one delivery format to focus on for the next 90 days. Let that be your main "proof & progress" lab.

Next, let's dive into a personal lens centered around our everyday life. To begin, we acknowledge that we are simply a human being juggling many hats. Yet change is still possible. In fact, there is proof it has already begun.

For Individuals: The Personal Breakthrough

Here is the Proof:

You create a life where actions match values. Your calendar reflects true priorities, not constant overcommitment and overwhelm. Beyond aligned living, you find a balance that integrates personal authenticity with professional excellence. You have found sustainable fulfillment rather than cyclical achievement. In turn, this influences others toward more intentional, purposeful approaches to success.

This is their Power:

You can say no without guilt and yes with clarity. You own your story and your growth. Beyond establishing personal boundaries, you discover self-leadership that models authentic success for others. In turn, these challenge inherited definitions of achievement, which opens the door to ripple effects of transformation.

This is their Progress:

You have discovered momentum without burnout and confidence without comparison. Your peace is aligned and full of purpose. Beyond individual peace, your approaches to growth create lasting transformation rather than temporary improvement. This, in turn, inspires others to question their own limiting patterns. Therefore, your impact contributes to collective evolution and encourages others to find more sustainable, authentic ways of living and working.

To see what this proof, power, and progress looks like in real life, consider the evidence that Marcus Thompson, a senior marketing director, discovered as he transformed his approach to his career and life integration. Traditional success metrics showed impressive results. He was promoted to VP level, earned a salary increase, and improved his work-life balance. But the real proof came at a systematic level. He fundamentally transformed his relationship with success, achievement, and personal fulfillment.

As a result of working with us, Marcus upleveled his individual leadership development. Marcus didn't just advance his career; he redefined what career success could include. Instead of climbing traditional corporate ladders, he created innovative value that elevated entire departments. Instead of competing with colleagues, he fostered collaborative excellence that strengthened team performance. Instead of sacrificing personal values for professional advancement, he integrated authenticity with achievement.

Marcus' power didn't sit in his individual success alone. He widened it to be defined by his influence on organizational culture. His department became known for innovation and collaboration. Other leaders began adopting his approaches to team development. His work-life integration became a model that HR began promoting organization-wide. He proved that individuals implementing the **S.P.A.R.K. Framework™** don't just achieve personal success, they influence organizational transformation from wherever they are positioned.

Marcus's story isn't about perfection, it's about alignment. He didn't quit his life and start over. He changed how he was living *inside* the life he already had.

Marcus Thompson: Proof, Power, Progress Snapshot

	In His Story (Example)	**Transformation To Look For in Your Life & Career**
Proof	He advanced in title and compensation *and* improved his work–life integration. His schedule, energy, and relationships reflected his genuine values.	Your calendar, boundaries, and energy start to look more like the life you desire—versus the life you've fallen into.
Power	He stopped chasing traditional ladders to create innovative value that lifted entire departments. He did this while staying grounded in his own definition of success.	You make moves based on what's right for you and those you serve—not just what "looks good on paper." You can say, "This is success *for me*." without apology.
Progress	His personal transformation quietly reshaped his department's culture. HR used his approach as a model. His growth changed the system around him.	People around you change because you have. Your choices inspire others to adjust how they work, lead, or live. Your growth shows up in the room, not just in your journal.

Now it's your turn to design the life you yearn for.

It is time to go beyond chasing a job title or a role on an org chart and become an individual who operates from a place of wholeness, fully aligned to the life you want. To begin, use the questions and first steps below to start creating your own proof, power, and progress in real time.

What You Want to Create	Questions to Ask Yourself	Simple First Steps (Personally & In Your Life)
Proof – which includes living a life that reflects what matters most to you.	• Where does my calendar reflect my true values and where does it reflect other people's expectations? • What recent decisions make me feel most like myself? • When do I say "yes" when my body, mind, or spirit clearly says "no"?	• Pick one value (family, health, creativity, faith, impact, rest). Protect one block of time to dedicate to it this week. • Do a 10-minute "calendar audit." Circle events that feel aligned; underline what feels draining. • Change or cancel one obligation that's clearly misaligned. Note how you feel afterward.
Power – which comes from an inner authority that isn't controlled by comparison or approval.	• When do I wait for permission to make a change I already know I need? • Whose opinion do I silently prioritize over my own wisdom? • What story about my worth or potential am I ready to stop repeating?	• Finish this sentence in your journal: "If I fully trusted myself, I would…." List 3 things without editing. • Set one small boundary this week (response time, availability, emotional labor). Honor it at least once. • Unfollow or mute 3 accounts that trigger comparison in your mind. Replace them with voices that ground and inspire you.
Progress – which includes momentum without burnout, and movement without self-betrayal.	• What does *sustainable* growth look like for me? • When have I confused being busy with moving toward what I want? • What next step can I take which feels honest and doable—versus heroic and impossible?	• Choose **one S.P.A.R.K. Framework™**-aligned goal (personal or professional) and define the *smallest* next step you can take in 15–30 minutes. • Schedule a weekly "check-in" with yourself. Ask, "What moved? What drained me? What did I learn?" • Celebrate one win every week. This might mean celebrating a decision you made, a boundary you honored, or a pattern you interrupted. This goes in your personal "progress log."

The S.P.A.R.K. Framework™ Reflection: Proof, Power, Progress

Take a moment to pause and answer:

Where can you clearly see the proof of your progress?

____

____

How does this proof represent systematic transformation rather than improved performance within existing limitations?

____

____

How has your understanding of power shifted through this journey?

____

____

How does your current relationship with power challenge inherited assumptions about authority, influence, and leadership effectiveness?

____

____

Define one area where you're ready to stop playing small and lead with bold progress.

____

____

How can this progress create ripple effects that impact systematic change beyond your immediate sphere of influence?

____

____

Make sure you scan the QR code at the end of this chapter to access free downloadable resources and micro-learnings and continue to evolve! You're no longer waiting for change. You are the change.

Now is your time to move forward faster!

The evidence is undeniable. The proof is everywhere. The power is yours. The progress is systematic. And the future? Well, the future belongs to leaders like you who understand that transformation isn't just about individual successes, it's about systematic change that creates fresh possibilities for everyone for long term and repeatable results.

This is why Brown Transformations Consulting exists. We are here to support leaders and organizations who are ready to become proof that systematic transformation creates exponential impact. To provide the expertise, accountability, and strategic guidance needed to ensure your individual breakthrough becomes collective revolution. We help you to measure and communicate the systematic change you are experiencing so your influence extends far beyond what you ever imagined possible.

You've seen the **S.P.A.R.K. Framework™** in action but now comes the most important part. Now you get to live it! In doing so, this shift becomes identity. It is where your rise becomes your new standard.

You may not feel "finished" (*you're not supposed to*). You may not see all your proof yet (*that's still unfolding*), but you *have* something you didn't have before. You have earned language, clarity, and a redefined framework to recognize and create transformation on purpose, repeatedly.

The question now is not, *"Does the **S.P.A.R.K. Framework™** work?"*

The question is,

"Who do I become when this is no longer just a framework I understand, but the way I live, lead, decide, and design my future?

Quote to Close the Chapter:

Transformation doesn't announce itself with trends—it reveals itself through consistent, systematic evidence that what once seemed impossible has become inevitable. You are that evidence. Your progress is that proof and your leadership is that power.

— Dr. Michelle Brown

SCAN TO TAKE The S.P.A.R.K. Framework **Assessment™**

Next Up: Chapter 11 – Your S.P.A.R.K. Shift: Embody The Framework, Empower The Future

In the final chapter, we'll step into *embodying* it so it shows up in how you lead at work, how you live at home, how you navigate change, and how you continue building what's next. If you're ready for real transformation, turn the page and dive into the final step to becoming the leader the future is waiting to see fully emerge!

CHAPTER 11 – YOUR S.P.A.R.K. SHIFT
EMBODY THE FRAMEWORK, EMPOWER THE FUTURE

You've done more than just read a book; you've initiated a shift. You've not only met the **S.P.A.R.K. Framework™**, but you've also activated it, tested it, and reflected with it. Now comes the most powerful part. You get to embody it.

Your **S.P.A.R.K. Framework™** shift isn't just a mindset; it's a model for how you move in the world. This is your road map for how you will lead, live, grow, decide, build, recover, rise and still ignite others along the way. Beyond individual embodiment, this rise is about becoming a systematic transformation catalyst who redefines what's possible in every room you enter. This is about shifting from someone who adapts to outdated internal systems to someone who replaces faulty internal systems with sustainable, holistic alternatives.

This holistic shift isn't abstract, it's built from earned skills, mental muscles, and the choices you've made along the way, personally and professionally.

You've discovered:

1. How to root yourself in **[S]**trategy. You don't lead in circles.
   > Beyond strategy, you have developed systematic thinking that challenges assumptions while building adaptive capacity for the future.

2. How to build a **[P]**lan that supports vision, not just tasks.
   > Beyond organizing labor, you have learned how to create adaptive frameworks that honor individual authenticity and organizational effectiveness.
   > You have replaced rigid structures with sustainable internal systems.

3. How to take aligned **[A]**ction, even when things are messy, challenging, unknown and uncertain.
   > Beyond initiating motion, you now know how to implement transformation that challenges comfortable patterns while building breakthrough possibilities.

4. How to track **[R]**esults that reflect real progress, not just surface level performance optics.
   > Beyond metrics, you now know how to measure change versus just activity.
   > You celebrate evidence of root level shifts rather than clapping for elevated performance numbers within harsh limitations.

5. Lastly, how to turn **[K]**PI Knowledge into power that drives lasting sustainable and replicable change, not high turnover and burnout.

    Beyond gathering data alone, you now know how to develop systematic intelligence that exposes opportunities while challenging frameworks that limit authentic progress.

From here, the invitation is simple but transformational. Leverage the **S.P.A.R.K. Framework™** until it becomes your way of life, not just a tool you refer back to occasionally. Let it challenge you in your calendar, conversations, goals, pivots, and day-to-day legacy. It is worth it to let it be your anchor. Why? Because sustainable transformation is not about doing more; it's about doing only what aligns, over and over again, until alignment becomes the standard and leadership becomes the sole core of who you are, personally and professionally. Your integrity.

Beyond personal embodiment, this framework is an invitation to contribute to collective **CoEvolution™**. It has the power to influence every internal system you touch, every organization you impact, and every person you encounter. Leaders who redefine industries and create breakthrough possibilities go beyond implementing better personal practices. Instead, they systematically transform how leadership functions across entire sectors, teams, and personal lives. Take a look below to see exactly what this looks like, once you make the **S.P.A.R.K. Framework™ Shift**.

Your S.P.A.R.K. Framework™ Shift is visible when:

1. A tough decision doesn't knock you off course from your purpose.
    - Instead, tough decisions become opportunities to demonstrate your strategic thinking in a way that influences others toward more authentic, sustainable approaches.

2. A setback becomes a moment of feedback, reflection and pivot, versus sinking into the feeling of failure.
    - Instead, setbacks become learning opportunities which strengthen your approach while also creating intelligence that benefits everyone in your sphere of influence.

3. A team meeting becomes a space for honest reflection and strategy, not just orders and tasks to complete with no clarity or goal in sight.
    - Instead, your approach to collaboration begins to transform how your team approaches collective intelligence and shared decision-making.

4. Your daily choices start to reflect your highest goals. Your consistent choices model what authentic success looks like.
    - In turn, this influences others to question inherited definitions of achievement.
    - They have permission to explore more sustainable approaches to professional and personal fulfillment because of your example.

5. You're not guessing anymore, you're grounded. This means you are operating from systematic intelligence that can navigate any challenge while maintaining authentic purpose.
    o Your approach influences others toward more strategic, less reactive ways of operating.

6. You're not reacting anymore; you're rooted in clarity.
    o Beyond personal clarity alone, your systematic approach to challenges shifts how others in your circle approach uncertainty, conflict, and change.

7. You're not stuck anymore, you know what phase to return to when you need to recalibrate, refocus, and realign.
    o This personal agility is important, but there is more. Your systematic approach to continuous evolution becomes a model that others study and adopt. Therefore, your rise creates ripple effects of positive change that extend far beyond your immediate influence.

When a **S.P.A.R.K. Framework™ Shift** is embodied systematically—transformation becomes a lifestyle.

S.P.A.R.K. Framework™ Shift Reflection: Your Living Legacy

What does embodying a **S.P.A.R.K. Framework™** shift look like in your day-to-day?

____

____

How does this embodiment challenge outdated internal systems while building sustainable alternatives in each environment you enter?

____

____

Which habit or decision most reflects your transformation?

____

____

How is your transformation influenced by systematic change in your organization, industry, or community?

____

____

Who has noticed your growth, and what did they say?

____

____

How have others adopted or explored your approaches to leadership?

____

____

How will you keep the **S.P.A.R.K. Framework™** alive when momentum fades?

____

____

What systematic approaches will you implement to ensure continuous evolution rather than reverting to inherited patterns of limitation?

____

____

What legacy are you building?

____

____

How does this legacy contribute to systematic transformation that will benefit others for generations to come?

____

____

The Future Belongs to S.P.A.R.K. Framework™ Leaders

The future belongs to...	Motivational reminder
Leaders who treat their personal inner work as true strategy, not an optional task.	*"When I grow, my leadership grows with me—and everyone around me feels the difference."*
Organizations that integrate technology with humanity, not one at the expense of the other.	*"Our tools should amplify our people, not replace their value."*
Leaders who are willing to question inherited internal systems—even when those systems feel familiar or "safe."	*"Comfort is not the same as alignment. I choose what is right over what is easy."*
Teams who build cultures of psychological safety, accountability, and honest feedback.	*"We don't just work together—we grow together."*
Industries that evolve beyond "this is how it's always been done" into "this is what truly serves people *now*."	*"Tradition can inform us, but it will not confine us."*
Leaders who measure what matters, including human impact, systemic change, and sustainable results.	*"If I want different outcomes, I must honor different metrics."*
Professionals who refuse to shelf their humanity at the office door.	*"I am not a role—I am a whole human. My wholeness is my power."*
Decision-makers who are brave enough to say, "The old way isn't working. It no longer serves our people or our future."	*"My courage to tell the truth is a doorway to our next level."*
Coaches and consultants who build frameworks that create real transformation, not just impressive presentations.	*"I'm not here to perform. I'm here to create lasting change."*
Leaders like you who embody **S.P.A.R.K.** in real time, in real rooms, and with real people.	*"I am the proof that a different kind of leadership is possible—and I'm just getting started."*

Let me remind you: You are not waiting for the future of leadership to arrive, you are actively building it with every aligned decision, transformed internal system, and human-centered move you make.

The future belongs to leaders who see their individual transformation as inseparable from systematic change. When organizations integrate technological efficiency with human-centered values and industries evolve to serve with authentic purpose, we usher in that future. That outlook is being lived right now. Such a future is not abstract or far away, it's being built by those willing to embody systematic change rather than bolt new tactics onto old internal systems. Leaders like you understand that the greatest risk isn't challenging outdated approaches, the greatest risk is maintaining internal systems designed for a reality that no longer exists in the world we live in today.

This is why your **S.P.A.R.K. Framework™** shift matters beyond your individual success.

Your embodiment of the framework creates ripple effects that can influence entire industries. Your commitment to transformation contributes to collective evolution. It is what provides more sustainable, authentic, effective approaches to leadership and organizational development.

Just know, you do not have to do it alone. Our team at Brown Transformations Consulting is seeing amazing things happen across industries. We exist to support leaders, to ensure that their individual transformation creates the systematic change they are seeking. Our goal? We want each leader and organization we work with to experience personal breakthrough that becomes a holistic organizational revolution. We believe each individual's authentic success influences entire industries toward more sustainable, human-centered approaches that honor both individual fulfillment and collective effectiveness.

You are not just improving your own experience—you are upgrading the experience for everyone who comes after you. You are not just solving your own challenges—you are creating internal system alternatives that others can study, adopt, and build upon for years to come long after you're gone. You get to do more than just achieve personal success—you have what it takes to prove what's possible when authentic purpose meets strategic implementation rooted in human-centered focus. When human-centered approaches integrate with technological efficiency, transformation drives organizational revolution.

Your **S.P.A.R.K. Framework™ Shift** is your contribution to the future. Your embodiment of the framework is your legacy. The systematic transformation you have experienced is your gift that you get to extend forward to every leader, organization, and industry that follows in your footsteps.

A Redefined Era of Leadership

The way I see it, leadership has entered an era of redefinition. What once allowed organizations to survive will no longer be enough to help them thrive. The demands of this moment are clear. Leaders must embody a new way of leadership traits like the **S.P.A.R.K. Framework™**, as a way of being in order to ride the waves of change we all face.

This isn't theory—it's real transformation in action.

Today's leaders are being measured by more than titles, positional power, or short-term wins. We are each being judged by our ability to empower, inspire, and ignite sustainable internal systems that outlast the uncertainty around us and generational requirements from emerging professionals. The distinction between *traditional leadership* and the

S.P.A.R.K. Framework™ *leadership* is no longer subtle. The distinction between organizations stuck in survival mode and those pioneering the future via thriving practices is clear.

Let's take one final look at what characteristics define a **S.P.A.R.K. Framework™** leader, including the traits they embody, the mindsets they adopt, the emotions they regulate, and the transformation they create. Use this as both a mirror and a map. Let it reflect where you currently stand and guide you to lead authentically in this redefined era of leadership.

What a S.P.A.R.K. Framework™ Leader Embodies

<u>Dimension</u>	<u>S.P.A.R.K. Leader Embodiment</u>
Core Traits	Visionary, Authentic, Empowering, Resilient, Accountable
Mindset	Growth-oriented, Strategic, Innovative, Systemic Thinker, Human-Centered
Emotional Presence	Grounded, Empathetic, Courageous, Confident, Compassionate
Leadership Style	Collaborative, Transparent, Adaptive, Influence vs. Control, Results-Driven
Decision-Making	Data-Informed + Intuition-Aligned, Agile, Inclusive, Fact-Based
Relational Approach	Builds Trust, Cultivates Belonging, Develops Others, Listens to Understand
Action Orientation	Proactive, Purpose-Driven, Bold in Change, Consistent in Execution
Results Focus	Systematic Transformation, Lasting Impact, Collective Success, Continuous Improvement
KPI Alignment	Balances Quantitative + Qualitative Metrics, Measures What Matters Most, Connects Results to Legacy
Energy and Presence	Inspires Hope, Sparks Innovation, Remains Calm Under Pressure, Models Well-Being

Remember, leadership isn't a title, it's a way of being!

Now that you've experienced each pillar of the **S.P.A.R.K. Framework™**—**[S]**trategy, **[P]**lanning, **[A]**ction, **[R]**esults, and **[K]**PI Knowledge—you're ready to thrive with it.

The world is shifting and so is the standard for leadership. We get to embody human centered and consumer-powered transformation that lasts.

The S.P.A.R.K. Framework™ Ignited: Your Transformation Journey Continues

Congratulations! You've completed *The **S.P.A.R.K. Effect**™: Redefining Leadership for the Future*. This isn't an ending; it's your expansion point. From here, you get to host systematic transformation that influences every environment you enter, every organization you impact, and every leader who observes your approach to success. Your journey with the **S.P.A.R.K. Framework™** has just begun. The question isn't whether you're ready to lead, it's whether you're ready to redefine what leadership can accomplish when it is grounded in your truth, human-centered focus and care, authentic purpose, systematic intelligence, and unwavering commitment to transformation. This is your moment to discover individual fulfillment and lead collective breakthroughs you can see and feel.

The future belongs to leaders like you, and it starts now!

Closing Quote to Ignited Insight

"The future belongs to leaders who understand that individual breakthrough is the beginning of systematic transformation, not the end. Your transformation is not your destination; it's your contribution.

— Dr. Michelle Brown

ABOUT THE AUTHOR

Dr. Michelle Brown is not your typical leadership voice—she's a bold strategist, industrial and organizational psychologist, and the creator of the **five-pillar S.P.A.R.K. Framework Assessment™**, a transformative ecosystem for leaders who are tired of surface-level solutions and ready to replace habitual leadership with intentional, scalable impact. As an expert and PhD of Industrial and Organizational Psychologist, this is exactly what her field was designed for—understanding the internal systems that drive people, performance, and organizations forward.

Born and raised in Southern California, Dr. Michelle Brown is the eldest of six siblings, a devoted mother of two, and a proud wife to Patrick Brown Sr. As a first-generation college student and Division I scholarship athlete, she earned All-American honors playing softball—a game that demanded foresight, strategy, and grace under pressure. On the field, where every moment carried unpredictable outcomes, she learned how to think ahead, adapt quickly, and lead with clarity and ease—skills she now brings to every boardroom and consulting engagement.

She holds a bachelor's degree in psychology, a master's degree in Organizational Leadership, and a doctorate in Industrial and Organizational (I/O) Psychology, equipping her with the academic rigor and behavioral insight to drive systems, behavioral changes and individual transformation. Known for challenging outdated leadership models and calling for a bold, human-centered shift, Dr. Brown fuses behavior-based executive coaching, strategic consulting, and narrative-driven transformation to dismantle performative leadership and rebuild cultures of trust, clarity, and action. Her five-pillar **S.P.A.R.K. Framework™**—**[S]**trategy, **[P]**lanning, **[A]**ction, **[R]**esults, and **[K]**PI Knowledge—drives measurable progress and long-term results across industries.

With having trained over **50,000 professionals and 380 plus organizations** served, Dr. Michelle Brown's approach isn't about checking boxes; it's about humanizing the workplace in streamlined ways that don't duplicate efforts, track the right metrics needed to grow and in ways that actually resonate and last! She equips **C-suite executives, people managers, L&D teams, universities, coaches, and scaling consultants** to structurally challenge outdated systems, realign their strategy, and lead with purpose, data-driven clarity, and sustainable impact.

As CEO of Brown Transformations Consulting, she helps organizations dismantle performative leadership models and ignite structure-powered progress. Her work isn't rooted in theory—it's grounded in real results. Dr. Brown doesn't teach performative leadership.

She dismantles it.

This book isn't something you just read; it's something you do! Dr. Michelle Brown challenges you to trade your comfort zone for true transformation and she provides the expertise to sustain it for the leaders of the future and your legacy. If you're ready to shift from reactive to radical, from burnout to breakthrough, from noise to clarity, and turn rhetoric into results; the **S.P.A.R.K. Effect™** will meet you there.